Thank
with
Pleasure Come Back

Misel [illegible]

"On the Country"

the Micmac of Newfoundland

Doug Jackson

edited by Gerald Penney

Harry Cuff Publications Limited, St. John's, 1993

Appreciation is expressed to the Canada Council for publication assistance.
The publisher acknowledges the financial contribution of the Cultural Affairs Division of the Department of Municipal and Provincial Affairs, Government of Newfoundland and Labrador, which has helped make this publication possible.

Canadian Cataloguing in Publication Data

Jackson, Doug, 1951-

On the country

Includes bibliographical references.
ISBN 0-921191-80-4

1. Micmac Indians -- History. 2. Indians of North America -- Newfoundland -- History. I. Penney, Gerald, 1951- II. Title.

E99.M6J33 1993 971.8'004973 C93-098613-X

ISBN 0-921191-80-4

Cover photo: Chief Reuben Lewis, Souliann and Ben Stride by A. C. Gathorne-Hardy, 1906. (Hand coloured by Manfred Buchheit)
Back cover: map detail from *Newfoundland and its Untrodden Ways*, J.G. Millais, 1907. (Overlaid on original photograph by J.F. Cuff)

Published by
Harry Cuff Publications Limited
94 LeMarchant Road
St. John's, Newfoundland
A1C 2H2

Printed by
Robinson-Blackmore Printing and Publishing Ltd.
St. John's, Newfoundland

Table of Contents

Preface

Shortly after Conne River's "recognition" as a native community in 1973 (under a federal/provincial agreement), federal funds were secured to research Micmac use and occupancy of Newfoundland. To begin the daunting task a 25-year-old university student from Pincher Creek, Alberta, was hired. Doug Jackson lived in Conne River from 1976 to 1981, collecting material from a variety of written sources and through extensive interviews. He recorded his findings in a 350-page typescript. While Jackson's findings were incorporated in a series of political and legal documents of the day, what was presumed to be the only copy of the manuscript was lost in a fire. A near-complete copy of the Jackson manuscript was brought to light by Josep M. Jeddore of Milltown in 1992 and was presented to then Chief Shayne McDonald.

In editing the manuscript, the order, content and argument of the original has been maintained. However, some of the rhetoric contained in the draft has been removed and an unfinished chapter describing the community of Conne River in 1980 and detailing the political developments in the 1970s has been excluded.

A brief note outlining the current status of the Miawpukek Band at Conne River has been appended, while footnotes containing bibliographic references to recent scholarly work pertaining to the Newfoundland Micmac have also been added.

Gerald Penney
St. John's

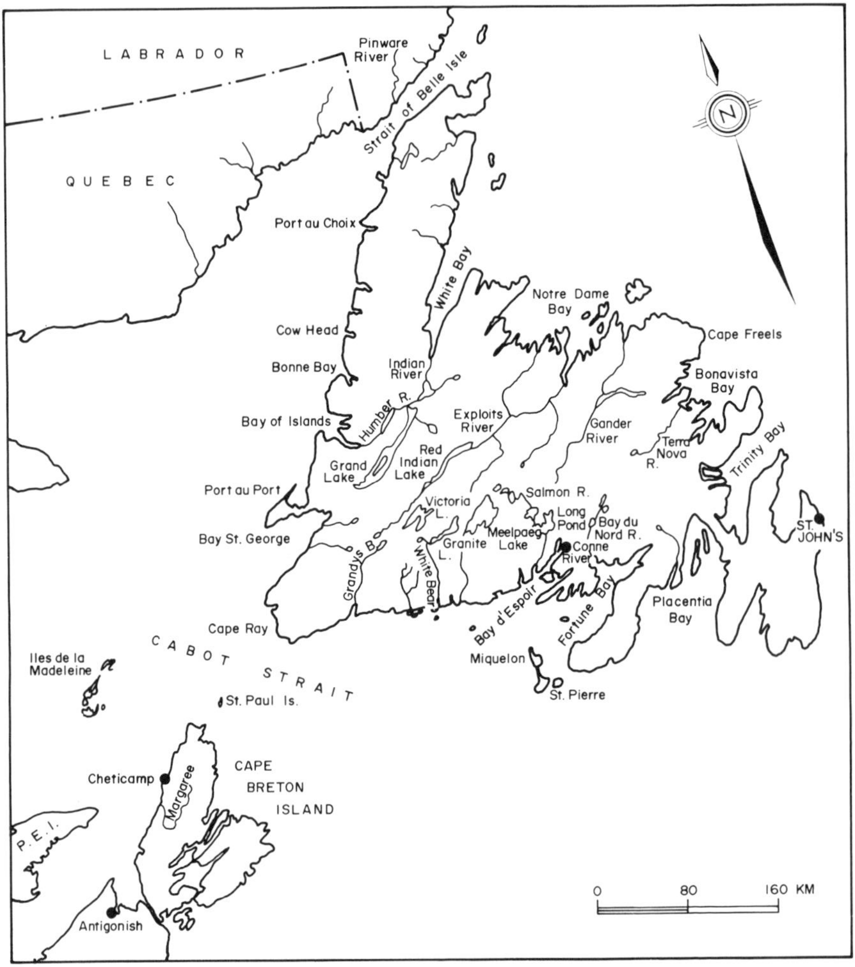

Newfoundland and Cape Breton.

“On the Country”

CHAPTER 1

Newfoundland prehistory — Question of prehistoric travel to island — Mode of travel — Reasons for migration

The prehistory of Newfoundland has been partially uncovered by archaeologists in recent years.[1] From their evidence it seems that the island was first inhabited 4000 years ago by an Indian people referred to as Maritime Archaic, immigrants from the continental interior. Beginning about 10,000 years ago, with the retreat of glacial ice, they migrated northeast, occupying both shores of the St. Lawrence, Labrador, and eventually Newfoundland, known to the Micmac as *Taqamkuk.*

Over the next millennium this parent population gave rise to several distinct offspring. The natural boundaries within their triangular area of occupation—Cabot Strait, the Gulf of St. Lawrence, and the Strait of Belle Isle—discouraged continuous contact among the dispersed groups and inhibited maintenance of a homogeneous culture. A gradual differentiation in language and lifestyle developed resulting in the emergence of several distinctive groups or tribes. It is assumed that from the Maritime Archaic people descended the historic tribes known as Micmac, Naskapi-Montagnais (or Innu), and Beothuk.*

Given a common origin, these tribes shared several basic cultural features. The classification in use among anthropologists today is the Algonquian family of tribes and languages. Their mutual isolation was only relative for the barriers which separated them were not insurmountable. After all, they had been bridged by their forefathers. Evidence from the early historical period suggests some degree of contact between the Montagnais and Beothuk across the Strait of Belle Isle.[2] Similarly the Micmac of Nova Scotia and Gaspé were known to visit Montagnais territory across the Gulf of St. Lawrence.[3] Whether such voyages were common during the prehistoric period is unknown.

Whether during the prehistoric period the Micmac undertook similar voyages to Newfoundland remains a matter of speculation. From the late 15th century on, European mariners sighted Indians on Newfoundland's shore, but we cannot be sure of their ethnic

---

*Ralph T. Pastore, *Shanawdithit's People: The Archaeology of the Beothuks* (St. John's, Atlantic Archaeology Ltd., 1992).

identity. Europeans of that era were not yet sufficiently familiar to distinguish between Indian peoples, commonly referring to them all as "savages." It is assumed that those sighted along the north and east coasts were Beothuk since this was their principal area of occupation.[4] Those observed elsewhere on the island are of uncertain origin. For example, according to various reports, Placentia Bay and White Bear Bay on the south coast and Bay St. George on the west coast were frequented by Indians during the 16th century.[5]

Some contemporary observers have argued that Cabot Strait, some 70 miles wide, posed far too hazardous a journey for prehistoric travel by birchbark canoe. Only after the acquisition of European sailing vessels (specifically shallops) could the Micmac attempt such voyages. They also maintain that, until the advent of English colonial settlement in Nova Scotia and Cape Breton and the subsequent depletion of wildlife resources, the Micmac had no reason to attempt the crossing.[6] There is no denying that the Micmac did adopt the shallop for ocean travel and that their migration to Newfoundland was largely driven by the impact of colonialism. Nonetheless the possibility of a prehistoric Micmac presence in Newfoundland cannot be dismissed. Judging from recent revelations concerning the migrations of other prehistoric peoples, modern writers consistently underestimate native navigational abilities.[7]

The Micmac were a maritime people adept in the construction and handling of canoes. One type of birchbark canoe was specifically designed for use on open water. It was a relatively large and sturdy craft over 20 feet in length and capable of handling considerable loads. Its most distinguishing feature was the contour of its gunnels, the midsections of which were raised several inches.[8] This design served to deflect waves in rough water, waves which would naturally tend to crest along the midsection. The Beothuk built ocean-going canoes of a similar design, and they were not averse to tackling the North Atlantic, travelling to and from the scattered islands of Newfoundland's northeast coast.[9]* While all other design elements of the Micmac and Beothuk canoe are identical with those of most other Algonquian tribes, the raised gunnel is uniquely theirs.

---

*See Ingeborg Marshall, *Beothuk Bark Canoes: An Analysis and Comparative Study*, Canadian Ethnology Series, Paper no. 102, 1985.

During the early historic period some writers spoke of the Micmac outfitting their canoes with sails. Whether this practice was aboriginal or European influenced has not yet been clearly established. One contemporary writer, an authority on Indian canoes in North America, suggests:

> . . . it is possible that the prehistoric Indians may have set up a leafy bush in the bow of their canoes to act as a sail with favourable winds. The old Nova Scotia expression ''carrying too much bush,'' meaning overcanvassing a boat, is thought by some to have originated from the Indian practice observed by the first settlers.[10]

W. E. Cormack's guide, Sylvester Joe, employed just this method to assist in crossing a large pond by raft during their expedition in 1822.[11] More recently the Micmac of Bay d'Espoir did the same with their canoes in navigating both salt water and fresh. Obviously the use of a sail would have been of considerable advantage in crossing Cabot Strait with its prevailing westerly winds.

French missionaries living among the tribe in the 17th century testify to the skill of the Micmac as navigators accustomed to making long journeys on open water, observing how they ''do not hesitate to paddle their bark canoes thirty to forty miles by sea.''[12] As another writer of that period marvelled, ''It is wonderful how these savage mariners navigate so far in little shallops, crossing vast seas without a compass, and often without sight of the sun, trusting to instinct for their guidance.''[13] Still another described how the ''Indians about Nova Scotia and the Gulf of St. Lawrence have frequently passed over to the Labrador, which is thirty or forty leagues,* without a compass, and have landed at the very spot they first intended.''[14]

Clearly then, the Micmac possessed the means and ability to cross the Cabot Strait, and the possibility also exists that they reached Newfoundland by an alternate route, across the Strait of Belle Isle from Labrador. A mere nine miles at its narrowest point, it could easily have been crossed either by foot on winter ice or by canoe after breakup. While Labrador was some distance removed from their traditional territory, there is evidence that tribesmen did occasionally visit, crossing the Gulf of St. Lawrence on hunting

---

*A league at sea is usually three nautical miles.

expeditions and on raiding parties against the local Montagnais.[15] While there is no direct evidence that any continued on to Newfoundland, it is possible considering the ease with which the trip could have been made. The Montagnais were known to frequent Newfoundland, and some remained and intermarried with the Micmac.*

In the absence of archaeological evidence about the possibly prehistoric origins of Newfoundland Micmac, a source of information is Micmac oral tradition. This is reflected in the work of Frank Speck, an American anthropologist who visited the island in 1914 to conduct ethnological research:

> Throughout Newfoundland the Indians [the Micmac] refer to their predecessors as *Sayewdjkik*, 'the ancients,' speaking of them as though they were the first inhabitants of the island. Some of the older Micmac-Montagnais even claim that the *Sayewdjkik* antedated the coming of the Beothuk. Ignoring such testimony, I think we may conclude that the term simply refers to the earlier Micmac colonists from the mainland, whose numbers were few and whose isolation rendered them distinct in some respects in culture and possibly in dialect. These peoples are believed to have been true Micmac and to have had a complete native nomenclature for the prominent places in the island. Some of the older Indians recall hearing about the last of these *Sayewdjkik* in the person of an old blind woman who died in Sydney many years ago. Although over one hundred years of age, she was conveyed in a canoe by her relatives, at her own request, over a large part of Newfoundland, giving the various lakes, rivers and mountains their proper names according to the ancient terminology. . . . The *Sayewdjkik* families are said to have become completely merged with the later comers from Cape Breton and Labrador.[16]

Though undoubtedly Speck was correct in discounting the assertion that the Micmac had preceded the Beothuk to Newfoundland, it would seem that the *Sa'qewe'ji'jk* had indeed resided on the island for a very long time. These 'later comers' were probably the immigrants of the 18th century, a period during which the major movement of Micmac to Newfoundland took place. If their predecessors had in fact been isolated from fellow tribesmen on the

*See Charles A. Martijn, "Innu (Montagnais) in Newfoundland" in William Cowan, ed., *Papers of the Twenty-First Algonquian Conference* (Ottawa, Carleton University, 1980), pp. 227-246.

mainland for a period of time sufficient to have "rendered them distinct in some respects," their migration could easily have been prehistoric.

As to how their forefathers had reached Newfoundland, Speck's informants asserted that they crossed the Cabot Strait by canoe:

> The route lay between Cape North (of Cape Breton) and Cape Ray on the southwestern coast of Newfoundland, a distance of sixty-five miles, land being dimly visible in fine weather. This bold journey was ordinarily accomplished in two days, they say.

On the first day—or night, since the sea is generally calmer then—the party of canoeists would set out for St. Paul Island roughly 15 miles off Cape North. Appropriately enough the Micmac had named this *Tuywe•'gan nmikuk*, "temporary goal island." Here the voyagers camped until the weather was favourable. Then an advance party of "three sturdy canoemen" continued the journey, paddling the remaining distance to Cape Ray:

> Landing here, they would await another calm night, then build an immense beacon fire on the highlands to serve both as a signal for advance and a guide for direction through the night.

The rest of the party would thus complete the journey:

> In affirming the testimony regarding this difficult accomplishment, Frank Paul of the St. George's Bay band, stated that the Indians occasionally, even in more recent times, went across, using bark canoes, in this way to Cape Breton. . . .[17]

Why these ancients immigrated to Newfoundland is speculative. Throughout North America the history of many Indian tribes is one continuous tale of migration and counter-migration, a tale sometimes preserved in their oral traditions, sometimes uncovered through archaeological research. Generally this ebb and flow of Indian peoples across the continent was driven by a combination of demographic, ecological and political factors.

The prehistoric Micmac of Nova Scotia, New Brunswick, Prince Edward Island and Gaspé were effectively hemmed in by neighbouring tribes to the north, west and south. Their legends speak of a long and bitter war with one such neighbour, the Mohawk, a powerful branch of the Iroquois confederacy settled to the west.[18] A series of defeats in battle could have forced a population shift eastward to compensate for lost lands. Cape Breton, the nost heavily populated area within Micmac tribal territory, would have been the most vulnerable to the pressure of overpopulation. An influx of refugees displaced by the Mohawk could have forced a migration to Newfoundland to relieve that pressure. By all later accounts it is certain that the island could have absorbed such an immigration since the indigenous Beothuk were not numerous and had never effectively occupied the entire island.[19]

An ecological crisis resulting in a succession of poor harvests could have created that same pressure, the need to migrate in order to avoid starvation. Natural increases in the tribe's population could have forced an expansion of tribal territory. An additional factor may have been mere curiosity, a desire among the more adventuresome tribesmen to explore that land "dimly visible" to the east. Some day archaeologists may discover more about the prehistoric period and these mysterious ancients.

NOTES

1. For a concise and authoritative account of Newfoundland and Labrador's prehistory, see James A. Tuck, *Newfoundland and Labrador Prehistory* (Ottawa, National Museum of Man, 1976).
2. Ibid., p. 62.
3. Lt. Edward Chappell, Voyage of His Majesty's Ship **Rosamond** to Newfoundland and the Southern Coast of Labrador (London: J. Mawman, 1818), p. 77.
4. Most documented contacts between Beothuk and European during the early historical period were confined to this area. J. P. Howley, ed., *The Beothucks or Red Indians*, Facsimile edition (Toronto: Coles Publishing, 1974), pp. 1-61, originally published by Cambridge University Press, 1915. Various implements, skeletons, and other evidence of prehistoric habitation uncovered elsewhere on the island, though commonly assumed to be Beothuk by observers of the 19th century, have in most cases been identified by archaeologists as Maritime Archaic or Palaeo-Eskimo.
5. J. D. Rogers, *Historical Geography of the British Colonies:* Vol.V – Part IV, Newfoundland, p. 29 (Oxford: Oxford University Press, 1911).
6. Ralph T. Pastore, *The Newfoundland Micmacs: A History of Their Traditional Life* (St. John's: Newfoundland Historical Society, pamphlet no. 5), p. 10.
7. For other examples: Celtic and Norse voyages to North America; Polynesian migrations throughout the South Pacific; the *Ra* and *Kon Tiki* voyages celebrated by Thor Heyerdahl.

8. Edwin Tappan Adney and Howard I. Chapelle, *The Bark Canoes and Skin Boats of North America* (Washington: Smithsonian Institution, *Bulletin* 230, 1964), pp. 58, 63.
9. Ibid., pp. 94, 98.
10. Ibid., p. 65.
11. Howley, *The Beothucks*, p. 143. "We occasionally crossed some of the large lakes on rafts, when our course lay across them and the wind happened to be fair, and there appeared nothing to induce us to go round their extremities. We accomplished this by fastening together three or four trunks of trees with withes, and held up a thick bush for a sail, and were blown over."
12. P. F. X. Charlevoix, *History and General Description of New France*, trans. J. G. Shea (Chicago: Loyola University Press, 1870) vol. I, p. 265.
13. Ibid., p. 264.
14. Bernard Hoffman, "The Historical Ethnography of the Micmacs of the Sixteenth and Seventeenth Centuries" (Unpublished PhD Dissertation, University of California, 1955), p. 146.
15. Chappell, *Voyage*, p. 77.
16. Frank Speck, *Beothuk and Micmac* (New York: Museum of the American Indian – Heye Foundation, 1922), pp. 123-124.

    In myths gathered among the mainland Micmac there are similar references to the *Sa'qewe'ji'jk*. Silas T. Rand, *Legends of the Micmacs* (New York: Longmans Green, 1894).
17. Speck, *Beothuk and Micmac*, pp. 119-120.
18. Hoffman, "Historical Ethnography," pp. 96-97.
19. According to James Tuck, an archaeologist at Memorial University, the aboriginal Beothuk numbered roughly 500. Pastore, *Newfoundland Micmacs*, p. 32.

CHAPTER 2

Micmac and Beothuk — First tribes contacted — Fur trade and European technology — Alliance with French — Placentia — Newfoundland hunting ground — French expulsion — Tickets of location — Encounters with naval governors

The Micmac were among the first Indian tribes in northeastern North America to encounter colonial Europeans. At the time they were a large and prosperous nation, roughly 6000 strong, occupying the whole of present-day Nova Scotia, Prince Edward Island, and a portion of New Brunswick and Gaspé.[1] By the close of the 18th century, however, the Micmac were a diseased, starving and landless people. Consequently some chose to seek sanctuary in Newfoundland.

The colonization of Micmac lands began in the early years of the 17th century when small contingents of French settlers established themselves in Acadia and Cape Breton. At this time the Micmac had been known to the French for some time. Contact had occurred over a century before, perhaps as early as 1504 when Basque fishermen were reported to have discovered Cape Breton. Over the intervening period the French developed an active fishery in the area, particularly in the late 16th century, by which time Newfoundland waters were becoming overcrowded.[2]

Contact with fishermen had one immediate and devastating effect upon the Micmac; namely, the introduction of disease. Smallpox, measles, whooping cough and tuberculosis — alien diseases against which the aboriginal had no resistance — all took their toll. By the close of the 16th century almost half of the Micmac nation had died off.[3]

A second consequence of contact was the introduction of European technology and the subsequent rise of the fur trade. For the French the development of trade with the indigenous population offered an obvious advantage. Ships' captains and individual fishermen could conveniently supplement each season's fishing voyage by returning home with furs as well as fish; furs like otter, fox and especially beaver, commanded a handsome price on the European markets. Ships' stores included a variety of goods—knives, axes, kitchenware, clothing, firearms and ammunition—to be offered in exchange for pelts.

This trade offered advantages to the Micmac as well, at least in the short term. Metal goods were more efficient and durable than bone, wood and stone implements. Eventually Micmac participation in the fur trade proved their undoing, for in the exchange their independence was unwittingly sacrificed. Once their traditional crafts were abandoned in favour of European goods, they quickly became dependent upon the trader for a continuous supply, particularly of metal goods, which in most cases they could neither manufacture nor repair. The exchange was irreversible, and in the process many craft skills were lost. The fur trade quickly emerged as a fundamental part of the Indians' economic system.[4]

The rise of the fur trade drastically upset traditional Micmac subsistence patterns. Prior to contact the bulk of their subsistence came from marine resources. Individual bands spent the better part of the year camped on or near the coast to hunt, fish and gather a tremendous variety of resources: seal, cod, flounder, smelt, salmon, various shellfish and shorebirds. Inland game like moose, caribou and bear provided an important but much smaller proportion of the yearly diet, usually harvested in winter when camps were shifted inland for brief periods. With the advent of trade, small fur bearers became the primary object of the hunt. Thus as individual families were forced to concentrate more and more upon the harvest of furs to support themselves and their families, the subsistence and settlement patterns of the tribe became radically reoriented towards the interior.[5]

Inevitably this revolution in lifestyle triggered an ecological crisis, a drastic reduction in fur-bearing populations, as the annual harvest of pelts steadily rose. Of the various species, beaver was the most vulnerable to over-trapping, for it was easily taken by the hunter and its pelt was the most highly valued. The inflated value of the beaver pelt astonished the Micmac, as one hunter remarked, "In truth, my brother, the beaver does everything to perfection. He makes for us kettles, axes, swords, knives, and gives us drink and food without the trouble of cultivating the ground."[6] Inevitably game stocks dwindled.

Big game suffered as well, with moose, caribou and deer taken in greater numbers since families had to support themselves in the interior for a much longer period than the traditional fall and winter months. In addition, a small but growing population of French settlers added pressure by either hunting themselves or outfitting local Indians to supply fresh meat. As a further disruption of the traditional lifestyle, during the summer months when the Micmac would otherwise be involved in the fishery, laying up provisions for the winter, they were now preoccupied with trade, conveying their season's harvest of furs to the French fishing stations and trading posts. By the middle of the 17th century the situation had become so critical that reports of starvation were common, particularly among the Micmac of Cape Breton.[7]

Undoubtedly it was this crisis which initially compelled the Micmac to seek new hunting grounds, but where? Adjacent lands to the south, west and north were occupied by other tribes, many of whom were similarly suffering. To the east, across the Cabot Strait, lay a sparsely populated island richly endowed with wildlife resources.

Newfoundland of the 17th century was more than a fishing station yet less than a colony. Since Cabot's time both France and England had expanded their fisheries, yet neither had made any consistent attempt to actually settle on the island. Each spring large convoys of ships sailed from Europe, only to return in the fall laden with codfish. They pursued the 'dry fishery' whereby the catch was salted and dried upon platforms or 'fish flakes' erected along the coast and, thus cured, freighted home. Permanent settlement was confined to a small number of 'planters,' as the English called them, a small fraction of the thousands engaged in the migratory fishery, who wintered over in tiny, isolated coastal villages. These English fishing 'stations' were distributed along the eastern shores of the Avalon Peninsula northward toward Bonavista Bay, the French in Placentia and Fortune bays, and along the eastern shore of the Great Northern Peninsula.[8]

References to the Micmac in early historical documents are fragmentary and somewhat vague. An English mariner, Bartholomew Gosnold, encountered a party of eight Indians aboard a shallop off the New England coast in 1602. When he asked for directions they "with a piece of chalke, described the coast thereabouts" and referred to "Placentia of the New-found-land."[9] Sometime earlier, in the 16th century, one of the first Jesuit missionaries to the Maritimes reported that "the small resident French colony in Newfoundland carried on trade with mainland Indians as far south as the Potomac.''[10] Sometime after Gosnold's voyage, the French explorer Samuel de Champlain reported that Indians from the mainland pursued trade with the French in Newfoundland.[11]

None of these sources identified these Indians as Micmac. They are assumed to have been Micmac since the encounters occurred in areas known to be occupied by the tribe. None of their references associating the Micmac with Newfoundland suggest a motive other than the pursuit of trade. Since there was ample opportunity to trade on the mainland, their movement to Newfoundland seems to imply an additional motive; namely, the pursuit of game and country lifestyle it offered.

The situation is clarified somewhat by another observer of the period. Jesuit missionary Pierre Biard, living among the Acadian Micmac, learned that they were indeed familiar with Newfoundland. In a 1616 report to his superiors he briefly described the population and distribution of the tribe:

> I have found from the Accounts of the (Acadian) Savages themselves, that in the region of the great river, from Newfoundland to Chouncoet, there cannot be more than nine or ten thousand people.[12]

Moreover, according to Father Biard, the French place name 'Placentia' was in fact derived from the Micmac word '*Presentic.*'*

From these scattered references, it is known that the Micmac had begun to extend their tribal territory to encompass Newfoundland by the beginning of the 17th century. How many crossed is not known, nor can it be determined if any settled permanently. During an initial period of expansion it is likely that hunting parties made seasonal trips, familiarizing themselves with the country, taking game over the fall and winter months, then returning in spring. No doubt any decision to remain depended upon the need to maintain a reliable access to trade goods. It appears that an ongoing trade was available with the French in Newfoundland.

No doubt there was considerable temptation to remain. Newfoundland offered an abundance of wildlife resources, in contrast to the depleted game stocks of Cape Breton. In addition it offered sanctuary from the ravages of colonialism sweeping through the

---

*See John Hewson "The Name *Presentic* and Other Ancient Micmac Toponyms," *Newfoundland Quarterly*, 1981-82, Winter, vol LXXVII, no. 4, pp. 11-14.

Maritimes. As the Micmac of the 17th century discovered, there was more to colonialism than the fur trade.

The economic dependence fostered by the fur trade was further strengthened by religious and political ties between the Micmac and emerging settlements. French colonial policy had one crucial objective, the protection of colonial possessions from the persistent threat of attack from New England. As long as France held Cape Breton and Acadia, she could deny England access to that 'great river,' the St. Lawrence, and thus protect Quebec. It was essential that local French authorities enlist and maintain the support of neighbouring Indian peoples, particularly the Micmac. As allies in arms they could help defend French settlements and participate in retaliatory raids against the English. Conversely, as enemies they could conceivably help drive the French into the sea. Thus, as the struggle for colonial supremacy intensified, the Micmac, for a time, held a balance of power.

French clergy played the key role in securing the alliance. Missionaries accompanying the first colonists were impressed by the local Micmac, judging them to be more "susceptible of civilization" than neighbouring tribes. They immediately began preaching among them.[13] In 1610 they gained their first convert, the legendary Membertou. Both a tribal chief and shaman, Membertou was an influential and respected leader. Following his conversion others followed suit; by the end of the century, the entire Micmac nation was Roman Catholic. Characteristically of the converted, they embraced the faith with an intense devotion, and became intimately bound to the French clergy, their new spiritual leaders. Given such leadership power the priests asserted a considerable influence over the Micmac, encouraging them to take up arms against the English who, being Protestant, were enemies of God as well as France. This alliance entangled the Micmac in the incipient "forest wars" at the periphery of New England and New France.[14]

Despite their vulnerability, the Micmac were by no means a subordinate partner. As long as they held the balance of power they exploited French fears that they might switch allegiance. In the hope of further solidifying the relationship, French authorities instituted a system of annual gift-giving whereby quantities of food, clothing, weapons and ammunition were distributed among the Micmac. On their part they accepted, indeed demanded, gifts as a form of tribute or payment for lands occupied and resources used. The upshot was that the Micmac, as one historian put it, "were able to play off two great powers against each other, while at the same time assuring a continuity of logistical support from one of them; no mean diplomatic feat in itself."[15]

It was a precarious balance. Hindsight judges it as a strategic ploy that was doomed to fail insofar as the struggle between the imperial powers intruded upon Micmac land. While the same colonial struggle would shortly encircle Newfoundland, and while the Micmac there would become similarly embroiled, the opposing colonial interests there were more concerned with fish than fur or farmland. The struggle there revolved around the land rather than upon it. Each spring convoys of French and English fishing vessels visited the coastal waters to reap the abundant cod, returning each fall with their catch. Over the years there emerged a mutual recognition of fishing grounds, with the French predominant in the south and the English along the east coast. Neither nation's settler population made any serious claim to the land, save the adjacent woods for supplies of fuel and building materials. Equally important to the Micmac, now firmly aligned with the French, the southern and western coastal areas immediately opposite their native Cape Breton remained either unoccupied or under French control.

France established her first and only major colony in Newfoundland in the 1660s. Fortifications were built at Placentia and a governor and garrison posted, though the population never numbered more than 400. References to Indians appear almost immediately. In the 1670s two English planters on the opposite shore of the Avalon Peninsula reported that, "Some Canida Indians from the Forts of Canida . . . have come over . . . to kill beaver and other beastes for their furres."[16] Presumably these were Micmac from Cape Breton, perhaps from the French settlement at Port Royal.

From Placentia Bay to Bay St. George the southern interior of the island was devoid of Europeans and perhaps only occasionally frequented by Beothuk. Like the Micmac, the Beothuk population by this point had been drastically reduced by disease; the survivors, by all evidence, were concentrated to the north, principally in the Notre Dame Bay area and the watershed of the Exploits River. The uninhabited wilderness of the southern interior offered an abundant variety of small game: fox, otter, muskrat and beaver. Thousands of woodland caribou roamed the bush and barrens. Fur and food were in abundance; trade goods were readily available from Placentia and the migratory fleets.

Wherever the Micmac established there was no escaping the outside world, the persistent warfare between France and England and the struggle for "new world" supremacy. As the struggle intensified, fellow Micmac on the mainland fought on, bound by history to the French and a losing cause. By the close of the 17th century Newfoundland became part of the battleground as well.

Placentia remained the only substantial French settlement on the island, "an isolated wayside inn on the highway from Paris to Quebec," as one historian put it, "little larger than St. John's, and only a little less than the entire French colony."[17] Important as the Newfoundland fishery was, France was more concerned with developing colonies elsewhere, especially in Quebec, where an expanding fur trade and rich farmland offered far greater profits.

The English, more by accident than design, had a greater stake in Newfoundland. Over the years a growing number of fishermen chose to abandon the annual migration and settle permanently, pursuing the fishery from small coastal villages. St. John's was one of over 30 communities that had sprouted along the rocky coastline from Ferryland to Bonavista. The English migratory fishery expanded steadily, encroaching on French interests. The migratory fleet was joined by privateers and men-of-war intent on harassing the French. Placentia, the wayside inn, became ever more vulnerable; her survival demanded an offensive.[18]

On three occasions—in 1696, 1705, and 1708—the French launched assaults on the English shore, burning and looting, in an effort to destroy England's colonial foothold. According to historical documents a number of

> . . . Canadian Indians took part in these attacks, supplementing the French expeditionary forces committed to the assaults. Some of the French had apparently recruited from among the Acadian Micmac and the neighbouring Abenaki tribe.[19]

It seems that most Indians, if not all, returned home shortly after French withdrawal. It is likely that some Micmac participated as guides on the march across the Avalon from Placentia to St. John's.

The most significant reference to the Micmac in Newfoundland was in 1705, when the French governor of Placentia reported the appearance of a party of about 20 or more families:

> It is their intention to establish themselves on this island which would certainly be very advantageous to them. The rest of their people are expected next spring, and I will do everything that I possibly can to see that they achieve their aims. I hope, Milord, for the good of the King's service and this colony, that you will agree to transfer here the annual presents that you send to their original territory, which they have left so that the animals which serve as their food supply can be replenished.[20]

The governor's report is revealing. His request for "annual presents" indicates a commitment to maintain the goodwill of the Micmac. There is nothing to suggest that he or French authorities had requested the presence of this band in Placentia; they were not imported as mercenaries! Nor does the governor speak of their appearance as unusual or unexpected, implying that others had visited Placentia previously or were known to reside on the island. The size of the band, perhaps over 100 in all, and the presence of women and children confirms that they were familiar with the island's interior and had already settled.

According to Governor Subercase, the band arrived in Placentia by land, presumably traversing the island from Bay St. George. As Subercase was told, there were more to come. In 1706 his successor, De Costebelle, reported a Micmac band wintering in Fortune Bay. A year later another band of 30 families, all from Cape Breton, landed at St. Pierre. That summer some of this group continued on to Placentia and wintered in Fortune Bay.[21] Apparently these families intended to return to Cape Breton but, as De Costebelle wrote, "They will find on this island a great quantity of caribou and beaver. I do not think that they will leave this place soon."[22] No doubt the abundance of game had tremendous appeal, a profound contrast to the impoverishment of their former hunting grounds. Here, too, there were no forest wars or land-hungry settlers to disturb the hunt. Save for winter forays across the Avalon, hostilities between England and France were exclusively naval.

Hostilities ended, at least temporarily, in 1713 with the Treaty of Utrecht. Under its terms France and England agreed that:

> The island called Newfoundland, with the adjacent islands, shall, from this time forward, belong of right wholly to Britain, and to that end the town and fortress of Placentia, and whatever other places in the said island are in the possession of the French, shall be yielded and given up. . . .[23]

What became of the Micmac in light of this treaty remains a bit of a mystery. Were they evicted from Placentia along with the French? Curiously, no Indian references appear in English or French records of the evacuation. As one historian describes the occasion:

> M. De Costabelle, the Governor, therefore lost no time in sending off the garrison and inhabitants to Cape Breton so that the latter might not lose their summer's fishing. Some of the people objected to leaving Plaisance [probably English and Irish servants] and would willingly have remained under English domination, but Costabelle urged all to go. . . .[24]

It is unlikely that the Micmac "would willingly have remained under English domination," considering the long-standing hostility between them. Similarly, it is unlikely that English authorities would have accepted a Micmac presence near their newly acquired fort. Presumably some Micmac retreated west in advance of the English occupation, shifting to Bay d'Espoir, Fortune Bay and points beyond.

English sovereignty over Newfoundland did not undermine Micmac occupation. Maintaining trade ties with the French may have proved awkward, given their withdrawal from Placentia and St. Pierre, but hunters could always convey their furs to Cape Breton, as many had done in the past. At the same time a French presence remained along the south coast. An English captain on one of the first patrols of the coastline, observed French fishermen and traders in the area, including a small village at Port aux Basques and a scattering of families in Fortune Bay.[25] Placentia Bay remained for some time devoid of English settlement, while on the west coast settler presence was confined to a small village in Bay St. George. England's failure to exploit the opportunities gained at Utrecht was partly due to a lack of adequate charts which, as Captain Taverner explained, "at present deters the English from sending their Ships to Fish and Trade there."[26]

A further deterrent was the presence of the Micmac. In 1727 a party was reported to have captured an English schooner anchored at Port aux Basques.[27] Six years later a naval commander patrolling the coast complained that "fear of those Indians" discouraged the development of an English fishery.[28] Fishermen were reluctant to settle in so isolated a region without assurances of protection. At this time the only English authority was an occasional patrol vessel such as Taverner's. From the Micmac point of view there was little to fear of the enemy; their position remained secure.

While the incident at Port aux Basques did arouse the concern of England's naval authorities, soon they were preoccupied with far more serious problems. By the 1740s peace collapsed and once again England and France were at war. During this, their second duel for supremacy in North America, the battles revolved around Cape Breton, Acadia and Quebec and had little bearing on Newfoundland. The Micmac were embroiled in the affair when, on two separate occasions, possibly at French instigation, they took a number of English prisoners. Both incidents ended in tragedy:

> In the fall of 1747 a party of some forty Cape Breton Micmacs wintering in Newfoundland (precisely where is a mystery) captured twenty-three prisoners and brought them back to Cape Breton where they were held until April of 1748.
>
> In that month, the Indians put twelve of their English prisoners in a boat with eight elderly warriors and their families and sent them to the St. John River where they were to await for the arrival of a larger group which was to take them to Quebec. The English prisoners, however, overwhelmed their captors and killed them all, men, women, and children. When the remaining members of that band learned what had happened, they slaughtered the eleven English captives which they still held.[29]

In the second incident English prisoners turned on their Micmac captors and killed 25.

It was this war which finally put an end to the Anglo-French struggle for North America. Under the 1763 Treaty of Paris, France was forced to "yield up" all her colonial possessions in the "new world," specifically New France (Quebec) and Cape Breton. The islands of St. Pierre and Miquelon, ceded in 1713, were returned to France with the proviso that they be maintained solely for the benefit of the fishery. Cape Breton was completely evacuated; the colonial authorities and garrison returned to France while many settlers, traders and missionaries went to St. Pierre.[30]

This change of circumstances proved disastrous for the Cape Breton Micmac. Their ties of friendship, faith and trade with the French abruptly severed, they now had to accommodate a new neighbour, the old enemy. Unlike the French, who demonstrated some respect for Indian culture and land, the English were not colonists but conquerors possessing full title to all lands.

During the American Revolution British loyalist refugees flooded into Micmac territory. Armed with government-issued grants, many chose to settle at coastal harbours and river mouths, locations which the Micmac favoured as summer and autumn campsites. Construction of sawmills and farms resulted in dammed streams and cleared forests, destroying the salmon fishery and pushing wildlife inland. Game populations, already reduced, were decimated by the settlers.[31] In a petition for government relief, one Micmac band complained of their destitution:

> In proof of this we need only remind you, that, during the deep snow last spring between two and three hundred Moose were taken by our white brothers in this small District alone. Other animals have been destroyed in nearly the same proportions, so that the food and clothing with which the Great Spirit so plentifully supplied us before the coming of our pale brothers is now cut off from our mouths and bodies and your red children left to inherit want and destitution.[32]

Such conditions were common throughout Nova Scotia and Cape Breton.

Impoverished, an increasing number were forced to turn to government relief. There was no longer a profit in trapping as encroaching settlement was despoiling trapping grounds. English authorities did attempt to revive the fur trade, establishing a series of "trucking forts," but the effort failed.[33]

To make matters worse, the Micmac were denied spiritual support. Their French priests gone, they became "very impatient and dissatisfied with the exercise of their religion," and petitioned for replacements.[34] On the advice of superiors, the English Governor ignored the request, fearing the return of French priests who could act as *agent provocateurs* and incite rebellion. Instead it was recommended that Protestant missionaries be recruited.

The English still feared the Micmac as a potentially hostile force. Immediately following the Treaty of Paris the British government formulated the Royal Proclamation, a statute intended to grant the Micmac a measure of protection against the loss of tribal land. However, the provisions and penalties of the proclamation were never properly enforced, the alienation of Indian land continued unchecked, and occasional hostilities arose.

Reports of widespread "poverty and destitution" among the Micmac aroused the sympathy of a few English observers, some of whom argued that certain lands ought to be set aside for their benefit. One such sympathiser was the surveyor general of Nova Scotia, Samuel Holland, a man well acquainted with the Micmac. In a 1768 report, Holland presents a clear picture of the issues and concerns, referring to a Cape Breton band encountered during the course of one survey:

> They behave very peaceably, but dissatisfied at the Lake being surveyed, saying we had discovered now all their private Haunts, which the French never attempted to do . . . it appears to me that their Chief Motive for assembling here is as they are mostly bigoted Papists, to deliberate upon what steps they shall take to get a priest among them, for which they are very anxious & frequently spoke to our surveying party in the Lake about it, & also mentioned they would be glad to have a Tract of Land along St. Patrick's Lake and Channel, granted them by his Majesty for the convenience of Hunting, and in which they might not be molested by any European Settlers.
>
> But as Jannot their Chief in this Island, was not yet returned from Newfoundland, to which place he went last Fall, they could not fix upon the Extent they would have, until they saw him. At present, they are greatly inclined to the French interest, but with a little Encouragement such as allowing them a Priest, a Number might be got to settle here who under the conduct of a Person of that Character, would be attached to our Government, & from the great Conveniency of Hunting around these Lakes it would be possible for them to carry on a considerable trade. . . . There still remains afterall, the Quantity of 808,000 Acres unapplied which I have titled the Savage or Hunting Country. . . . This however, if put to the Use the title implies, may be brought to great Value, by affording a Trade in Furs, with the Indians in Return for English manufactures.[35]

Holland's plan failed; no lands were set aside. Instead the government adopted the practice of issuing to Micmac leaders "tickets of location." Each ticket stated that a particular location had been traditionally occupied by the Micmac, and advised that it would therefore be ungentlemanly for any non-Indian to settle there. Since the tickets carried no force of law, they were seldom honoured.[36] The Micmac were unable to cope with the increasing number of colonists and the alienation of their lands.

It was against this backdrop of poverty and alienation that the major Newfoundland emigration took place. Without the benefit of a secure land base, the Micmac could no longer maintain tribal identity and independence. Some resigned themselves to their fate, while others like Jannot struck out in search of a better future. Over the closing decades of the 18th century, it is estimated that as much as half of the Cape Breton population crossed Cabot Strait.[37]

Colonial authorities in Halifax and Louisbourg were happy to bid them farewell. Memories of recent hostilities underlined a persistent concern that the Micmac might renew the conflict, especially in light of their grievances over land and religion. To assist in their departure the governor of Nova Scotia, Montague Wilmot, issued passports to several parties leaving for Newfoundland.[38] On one occasion during the American revolution, a colonial officer went so far as to offer a land grant as an inducement to resettle. As a later writer explains:

> During our war with America between the years 1775 and 1782, the Micmac Indians, inhabiting the Island of Cape Breton and the parts adjacent, were amongst the numbers of our most inveterate enemies; but at length one of our military commanders having concluded an amicable treaty with them, he selected one of the most sagacious of their chiefs to negotiate a peace. . . . The old Indian ambassador succeeded . . . and received as his reward the grant of a sterile tract of land in St. George's Bay, Newfoundland, together with permission to transport as many of his countrymen as might be willing. . . .[39]

If Governor Wilmot was eager to see these Micmac leave, his counterpart in Newfoundland, Thomas Graves, was hardly pleased to receive them. Again, there was the fear of renewed hostilities, especially in light of French presence on St. Pierre. Governor Graves feared that the Micmac would threaten the security of the emerging English fishery off the south coast. Graves learned of Micmac arrival when Captain Thompson of H.M.S. *Lark* reported intercepting a party in the neighbourhood of Cape Ray in the fall of 1763. Several of them "expressed a great desire to get to St. Peters to get a Priest, but this Captain Thompson . . . took all precautions he could to prevent."[40] Graves immediately wrote the home government suggesting that, "As their numbers are yet small, if gentle means will not confine them at Home, would it not be better to extirpate them from off this Island, than suffer such a connection to be kept up?"[41]

The connection with St. Pierre upset English authorities not only because of the security threat, but also because of the Indian trade monopoly enjoyed by the French. As Graves admitted to superiors in London, "I am afraid if they are not confined to their own side of the Gulf, it will be impossible to prevent their trading with the French."[42] The captain of another patrol vessel at Cape Ray reported that while the Micmac there had taken "large quantities of furs they sold only about 150 to our people; they went away with the rest early in the Spring for the Island of Cape Breton, but I suspect they found means of conveying it to St. Peters."[43] It would be some time before the Micmac would approach the English to trade. Later in the century a colonial administrator wrote:

> The Indians have for many years continually avoided coming near our settlements. The French have observed a very different Conduct towards them, and by Arts of winning the Affections of the Indians turned their Political Humanity to good Accounts, as I understand they have carried on a considerable Trade with them for Furs.[44]

Hugh Palliser, Graves' successor, was even more determined to sever the "French connection" and rid Newfoundland of the Micmac. In the fall of 1765, informed that a large party had recently landed on St. Pierre, he immediately dispatched two ships "to endeavour to send them away, as well as to protect our Fisheries."[45] The effort failed, as Palliser reported to the home government the following year: "I have now to acquaint your Lordships that 175 of those Indians, after having been at St. Pierre, landed in the Bay of Despair, and dispersed themselves about the country."[46]

Palliser was incensed to learn that these and other Micmac were issued passports by Governor Wilmot in Nova Scotia. He directed naval commanders to confiscate the papers and order all Micmac "to return to their own government."[47] In letters to Wilmot in Halifax and the garrison commander at Louisbourg, Palliser requested that all passports be recalled and no others issued. Wilmot presumed there had been a misunderstanding and in a letter to the commander explains:

> The letter from Mr. Palliser relating to the settlement of Mickmack Indians in Newfoundland has evidently arisen from some misrepresentation made to him—Jean Oulat, through a decent submission to the Authority of Government, applied for my leave to go over to the other Shore for the purpose of trading

> and hunting; had I refused my consent, which I could not with propriety have withheld, he might have taken that liberty with impunity, nor indeed can I find out the Law which prevents any of the King's subjects passing from any part of his dominion to the other. . . .[48]

As in Acadia under the Treaty of Utrecht, British colonial administrators held that all Indian inhabitants of former French colonies were to be treated as subjects of the Crown, a policy confirmed by Wilmot. As such they were clearly free to pass "from any part of his dominion to the other," like any other subject. Therefore, Palliser had no authority to either deport the Micmac already in Newfoundland or prevent others from coming. On the other hand, if in fact the Micmac were subjects of the Crown, there was no need to issue passports, as Wilmot had done, just as there was no law requiring them for Englishmen travelling from Cape Breton to Newfoundland. Wilmot's actions suggest that either he or his superiors did not consider the Micmac to be British subjects, but rather a separate nation.[49] The issue remained unresolved.

Whatever the legal status of the Micmac in Newfoundland, there was no escaping it. As Wilmot confessed, those remaining under his administration could leave "with impunity," while those already established on the island were firmly entrenched; as Palliser woefully admitted, he could only "despair of ever getting them out." Whenever confronted by English authority, they would withdraw to the interior and safety. They were here to stay.

Eighteenth-century Newfoundland remained a maritime colony—one giant fishing vessel anchored off the continental shelf, as many historians are fond of repeating. Fledgling settlements of the 17th century had grown slowly but steadily, extending north from the Avalon into Trinity and Bonavista bays and on to Notre Dame Bay. The migratory fishery reigned supreme, and transient fishermen outnumbered settlers. Despite the advantages gained under the Treaty of Utrecht, English settlement along the south coast remained marginal, totalling no more than 500 to 600 people by the 1770s, concentrated in Placentia Bay. During a survey in 1765, Captain James Cook did not find any settlements between Bay d'Espoir and Burgeo.[50]

Colonial settlement policy in Newfoundland was an expression of befuddled ambivalence. Administrative authorities and naval commanders were staunchly opposed, arguing that Britain's security depended on the primacy of the migratory fishery since it provided an effective "nursery for seamen." The powerful merchants of southwest England were opposed as well, fearing that a settler population would turn to the emergent continental colonies for "articles of manufacture," undermining their most profitable monopoly. On the other hand, the growth of a settler population was an established fact. Short of a costly and controversial eviction nothing would dislodge them. Proponents argued that their presence was a deterrent against French adventurism.[51]

In either case the primary concern remained the fishery. As one historian explains:

> The Newfoundland fishery then, offered the dilemma of an attractive resource available for such a short season that year-round habitation to exploit it was questionable; but on the other hand the location of the island, isolated as it was, made the logic of yearly migrations to it for the fish equally questionable. In the late seventeenth century and through most of the eighteenth century, both of these approaches were employed. Since each approach interfered with the other, there was an almost constant clash—sometimes physical—between the two schools of thought.[52]

All the dominant issues of the day which concerned colonial society and authority—the question of settlement, the treaty shore, and a host of others—focused on the fishery and had little bearing on the Micmac who turned "their backs to the Sea" and pursued a different life. Palliser's fierce opposition to their presence revolved around his concern with security, his fear of a renewed Franco-Indian alliance. Yet the French as a competing colonial power were gone from Newfoundland; on St. Pierre, their only remaining possession in North America, they were forbidden to locate military fortifications or personnel. The Micmac avoided contact with the English as best they could. As hunters and trappers they pursued resources in a land about which the English knew little and cared less. A certain measure of resentment over the French monopoly of trade with the Micmac was petty jealousy considering that neither Palliser, nor his predecessors, nor his successors made any effort to cultivate their trade. No doubt this antipathy was based in part on the Micmac participation in those raids on the Avalon (a memory which persists to the present day; even J.D. Rogers, an otherwise sympathetic historian, would write of the affair in a biased tone, referring to the Micmac crossing the Avalon "like a pack of wolves" attacking "like beasts of prey"[53]).

Whatever the nature of the antagonism, it was further aroused during Palliser's time by the emergence of quite a different concern. Reports reaching the governor alleged that the Micmac were threatening the security not only of English fishermen but of the Beothuk. This hapless tribe, it was alleged, was being harassed and hunted by the Micmac in a merciless war of extermination.

NOTES

1. Hoffman, "Historical Ethnography," pp. 112, 230.
2. Ibid., p. 16.
3. Ibid., pp. 228-231.
4. Ibid., pp. 31-32. Clear evidence indicating the development of the fur trade among the Micmac during the very early historical period is provided by Jacques Cartier. In 1534, decades before the actual colonization of Acadia, Cartier observed Micmacs in the Bay of Chaleur signalling his ship by waving furs to trade. H. P. Biggar, ed., *The Voyages of Jacques Cartier* (Ottawa: The King's Printer, 1924), pp. 48-51.
5. Hoffman, "Historical Ethnography," pp. 151-187.
6. Fr. Chrestien Le Clercq, *New Relation of Gaspésia*, William F. Ganong, ed. (Toronto: The Champlain Society, 1910), p. 277.
7. Hoffman, "Historical Ethnography," pp. 231-236.
8. C. Grant Head, *Eighteenth Century Newfoundland* (Toronto: McClelland and Stewart, 1976), pp. 2-13.
9. Gabriel Archer, "The Relations of Captain Gosnold's Voyages . . .," in Samuel Purchas, *Hakluytus Posthumus, or Purchas His Pilgrimmes* (Glasgow: James MacLehase and Sons, 1906), vol. XVIII, p. 304.
10. Reuben G. Thwaites, ed., *The Jesuit Relations and allied documents*, 73 vols. (Cleveland: The Burrows Brothers, 1896-1901), I, p. 177.
11. H. P. Biggar, ed., *The Works of Samuel de Champlain*, 6 vols. (Toronto: The Champlain Society, 1922-36), Vol. 3, p. 160.
12. Thwaites, *Jesuit Relations*, pp. 109-111.
13. Wilson D. Wallis and Ruth Sawtell Wallis, *The Micmac Indians of Eastern Canada* (Minneapolis: University of Minnesota Press, 1955), p. 11.
14. L. F. S. Upton, "Micmac Resistance in Nova Scotia, 1714-1740," (Unpublished paper, 1975), p. 6.
15. Ibid., p. 25.

16. Public Record Office (PRO), Colonial Office (CO), 1/38, Maritime History Archive, Memorial University, John Downing, "A Briefe Narrative Concerning Newfoundland," rec'd 24 November 1676.

    British Museum, Egerton MSS., 2395, Maritime History Archive, Memorial University, petition of John Matthews, 27 January 1670.
17. Rogers, *Historical Geography*, pp. 88, 89.
18. Ibid., pp. 90, 91.
19. Ibid., pp. 92-107.
20. Archives des colonies, Plaisance en Terre-Neuve, M.G.I., CIIC, Vol. IV, 22 Octobre 1795, pp. 321-322.
21. Ibid., vol. V, p. 253.
22. Ibid., vol. V, p. 209.
23. Cited in D. W. Prowse, *A History of Newfoundland from the English, Colonial and Foreign Records* (London: Macmillan and Co., 1895), p. 258.
24. Ibid., p. 259.
25. Rogers, *Historical Geography*, pp. 124-125.
26. CO 194/5/262.
27. Pastore, *Newfoundland Micmacs*, p. 12.
28. CO 194/23/180, Taverner to the Lords of Trade.
29. Pastore, *Newfoundland Micmacs*, p. 12.
30. Ibid., p. 13.
31. Harold McGee, "Ethnic Boundaries and Strategies of Ethnic Interaction: A History of Micmac-White Relations in Nova Scotia" (Unpublished PhD Dissertation, Southern Illinois University, 1974), p. 75.
32. Ibid., p. 76.
33. Elizabeth Anne Hutton, "Indian Affairs in Nova Scotia, 1760-1834," Nova Scotia Historical Society, Collections, vol. 34, 1963, pp. 36-38.
34. Public Archives of Nova Scotia (PANS), Record Group I, vol. 37, doc. 44, Governor Wilmot to the Board of Trade, 9 October 1765.
35. McGee, "Ethnic Boundaries," p. 72.
36. Ibid., p. 76.
37. Ibid., pp. 74-75.
38. Dennis Bartels, "Micmac Use and Occupancy of Newfoundland," (Unpublished paper, 1978), p. 15. Pastore, *Newfoundland Micmacs*, p. 14.
39. Chappell, *Voyage*, pp. 76-77.

40. CO 194/15/108, Governor Graves to the Board of Trade, 20 October 1763.
41. Ibid., p. 108.
42. Ibid., p. 108.
43. CO 194/17/27.
44. CO 194/43/263.
45. CO 194/16/302, Palliser to Lords of Trade, 21 October 1766.
46. Ibid.
47. Pastore, *Newfoundland Micmacs*, p. 14.
48. Governor Montague Wilmot to Col. Pringle, 22 December 1765, PANS, Record Group I, vol. 136, doc. 73.
49. Ibid.
50. Head, *Eighteenth Century*, pp. 159, 163.
51. Ibid., pp. 30-48.
52. Ibid., p. 30.
53. Rogers, *Historical Geography*, p. 92.

CHAPTER 3

Beothuk and Europeans — Extinction — Cormack's search — Cartwright's expedition to Exploits River — Micmac mercenary myth — Speck's Santu — Micmac and Beothuk relations

The fate of the Beothuk has been a topic of consuming interest for generations. The celebrated "Red Indians," a mysterious almost mythical people, have been extinct for over five generations; but why, at whose hands? The issue would be of minor interest were it not for the allegation that the Micmac were largely responsible; that these "Canadian Indians," ruthlessly set about exterminating the Beothuk. The allegation has no basis in fact but has been repeated since the last Beothuk died. Many subscribe to the myth; unjustly accused, the contemporary Micmac bear a burden of false guilt.

James Howley is one of the few authors who have written sensible and objective accounts of the Beothuk. A geologist, he spent over 40 years exploring and mapping the island's interior during the latter half of the 19th century. He had a unique opportunity to gather first-hand accounts of the Beothuk, both from settlers and from the Micmac. These and a host of other sources are included in *The Beothucks or Red Indians.*[1] Another reliable source is Frank Speck. A trained anthropologist and professional student of Indian affairs, he gathered information on the two tribes and assessed their historical and cultural relations in *Beothuk and Micmac.*[2] In addition three contemporary writers have written on the issue: Senator F. W. Rowe, politician, educator and author, has produced one of the most recent and sensible accounts, *Extinction: The Beothuks of Newfoundland*[3]; two historians, Professors L. F. S. Upton[4] and Ralph Pastore,[5] have each contributed informative articles.

At the time of contact the Beothuk were a relatively small tribe numbering between 500 and 1000, concentrated along the northeast coast of Newfoundland, especially in the Bay of Exploits. Like the aboriginal Micmac, they were a maritime people, subsisting for much of the year on marine resources, hunting inland in the fall.

Relations between the Beothuk and Europeans were characterized by hostility from the beginning. Leslie Upton traces the development of this relationship through three stages. "The first lasted from 1500 to 1612 and was marked by occasional kidnappings, casual trade, sporadic pillage, and mutual retaliation."[6] In contrast to the Micmac-French experience, the English made no concerted effort to establish commercial ties with the Beothuk. Once familiar with trade goods though, (and in the absence of a continuing trade), the Beothuk habitually raided the fishermen's shore facilities, salvaging various goods during the off-season and inviting retaliation.

This first period of contact was marked by the introduction of disease. By the end of the 16th century epidemics had reduced the Beothuk population to less than 500. Most observers agree with Rowe's assessment that it was this factor more than any other which led to their extinction.[7]

The last recorded instance of friendly contact was in 1612 when John Guy exchanged gifts with a party of Beothuk at Bull Arm, Trinity Bay. The following year that same party was met and fired upon without warning by the crew of another English vessel.* As Upton explains, "Never again did the Beothuk attempt to trade with the white man. They withdrew from all voluntary contact and remained hidden to the end." He describes the second stage "when the Beothuk withdrew into the interior to live beyond the restricted range of the European fishermen who visited the coast."[8] So too they withdrew from the written record, as did the Micmac of the southern interior, safe for a time from European intrusions.

The third and final stage as envisaged by Upton "began in the middle of the eighteenth century when whites moved in from the north coast to use the resources of the interior along the line of the Exploits River, the very area to which the Beothucks had withdrawn."[9] In addition to pursuing the inshore cod fishery in Notre Dame Bay, Europeans moved inland trapping and salmon fishing. Their penetration into the heart of Beothuk territory posed a critical threat to the surviving members of the tribe. Now forced even farther inland and denied access to coastal resources, the Beothuk were further reduced in number by starvation.[10]

Still they retaliated, harassing trespassers, raiding campsites, and pilfering sails, nets, traps, food, anything of interest or value.

---

*See William Gilbert, "Divers Places: The Beothuk Indians and John Guy's Voyage into Trinity Bay in 1612." *Newfoundland Studies*, 1990, Vol. 6, no. 2, pp. 147-167.

The settlers' response was often brutal. John Reeves, chief justice of Newfoundland, reported to a government committee:

> It seems very extraordinary, but it is a fact known to hundreds in the northern part of the island, that there is no intercourse or connection whatsoever between our people and the Indians but plunder, outrage and murder. If a wigwam is found it is plundered of the furs it contains, and is burnt; if an Indian is discovered he is shot at exactly as a fox or bear. This has gone on for years in Newfoundland.[11]

Early reports of this "outrage and murder" prompted Governor Palliser to take action, launching Lieutenant John Cartwright's 1768 expedition to the Exploits. The objective, in Cartwright's words, was to effect "a friendly intercourse with them, in order to promote their civilization, and render them in the end, useful subjects to His Majesty."[12] Accompanied by Tom June, a Beothuk guide, Cartwright penetrated as far as Red Indian Lake but failed to locate Beothuk. Reporting to the governor he describes the atrocities committed by the settler population. He includes the assumption that there was hostility between Micmac and Beothuk.

> These Indians are not only secluded thus from any communication with Europeans, but they are so effectually cut off from the society of every other Indian people. The Canadians have generally a strong hunt that range the western coast of Newfoundland, between whom and these natives reigns so mortal an enmity . . . that they never meet but a bloody combat ensues.[13]

Perhaps this was the original allegation of hostility between the two tribes, one subsequently accepted by Governor Palliser, his successors, and colonial society as a whole.

What evidence did Cartwright provide to substantiate his conclusion? On whose testimony does he base his reference to "so mortal an enmity"? No one's but his own presumption that such conflict "is the case with all savage nations; occasioned by mutual fears, and not being able to understand each other's language."[14] The allegation of inter-tribal enmity is a racist assumption.

Contrary to Cartwright's assumption, there is nothing inevitable or inherent about warfare among "savage nations." The most common cause of friction between neighbouring peoples is usually competition for resources or markets. Such was the conflict underlying the wars between England and France—for the fish, fur and farmland of North America—and that between the English and

Beothuk—for the fur and salmon of the lower Exploits. Cartwright seems to imply this.

> We know that the Canadians [the Micmac] range all the western coast opposite to those parts [the shores of Red Indian Lake]; and probably the same reasons prevail over them, that drive these savages [the Beothuk] into the interior parts of the country during winter.[15]

The 'drive' or motive which drew them inland was caribou, which they hunted as they crossed the Exploits River in the fall. The Micmac moved inland as well during fall and winter to take furs as well as caribou, but their hunting grounds lay far to the south of Red Indian Lake. It could be hypothesized that, had the Beothuk population not been decimated by disease, the influx of Micmac after 1763 might have resulted in hostile behaviour.

Colonial society accepted the allegation without question, and from 1768 onward, through correspondence and dispatches, we find the expression if not the conviction that the dwindling Beothuk were being further victimized by armed and hostile Micmac.[16] Yet no one at any time offered any evidence of a specific instance of aggression.

Given the Europeans' ignorance of the interior and events therein, only the Micmac and Beothuk themselves could shed any light on the question of their relations. The only member of either tribe Cartwright ever spoke to was his guide. What did Tom June have to say? He "related that the two nations did not see the least signs one of the other during whole winters," Cartwright reported. As far as the guide knew, the Micmac never penetrated farther than the western end of Red Indian Lake, while his own tribesmen kept to its eastern shores.[17] At worst June's evidence might suggest an antagonism of some sort, a result of some situation we do not know, an antagonism resolved through a policy of mutual avoidance. In the early 19th century there is additional evidence for peaceful or maybe agreeable division of tribal territory.

Following Cartwright's expedition, concern for the Beothuk mounted. The colonial government issued a proclamation condemning the settlers' reported "inhuman barbarity" and directing officers and magistrates to "apprehend all persons who may be guilty of murdering any of the said native Indians."[18] In 1807 Governor Holloway offered a "Reward of Fifty Pounds" to anyone who could induce a Beothuk "to attend them to the Town of St.

John's."[19] There followed a succession of expeditions up the Exploits; most ending in failure, succeeding only in thoroughly intimidating any Beothuk who chanced to see these large parties of heavily armed men.[20] A handful were captured, a few others gave themselves up in desperation, starving; all but one died shortly afterwards of tuberculosis. That lone survivor, the legendary Shanawdithit, lived to tell a pathetic tale of her people's suffering. Most alarming of all was her statement that there were only a dozen of the tribe remaining in the spring of 1823 when she was captured.

In 1822 Cormack launched his first expedition in search of the Beothuk, an ambitious crossing of the island's interior. The route Cormack selected, striking almost due west from Trinity Bay to Bay St. George, led somewhat south of the height of land separating the river systems flowing north and south. The fact that he met with Micmac rather than Beothuk along this route suggests that the Micmac confined themselves to the southern interior. Second, all those with whom Cormack spoke testified consistently that Beothuk territory lay to the north, specifically in the neighbourhood of Red Indian Lake where the tribe was then camped. As the Micmac explained the Beothuk were known to "occupy the Great or Red Indian Lake, and many other lakes in the northern part of the Island, as well as the great River Exploits."[21] Most important of all though, Cormack wrote, this "great division of the interior of Newfoundland is exclusively possessed and hunted over by Red Indians, and is considered as their territory by the others."[22] Clearly then there was an explicit division of tribal territory acknowledged and respected by the Micmac, as Tom June's testimony implied.

This was confirmed by Cormack on his 1827 expedition. His route ran northeast from the mouth of the Exploits to the head of Hall's Bay, west from there to Bonne Bay, due south to Red Indian Lake, then down the Exploits to salt water. As in 1822, Cormack was accompanied by Indian guides, three on this occasion, and again he failed to locate the Beothuk. As so many others had before, he found ample evidence of occupation, their wigwams and burial grounds on the shores of Red Indian Lake, but no recent sign.

> There were everywhere indications, that this had long been the central and undisturbed rendezvous of the tribe when they had enjoyed peace and security. But these primitive people had abandoned it, after being tormented with parties of Europeans during the last 18 years.[23]

Camped on the shores of this sanctuary Cormack again wrote of the tribal division of territory.

> I could not help observing that two of my Indians evinced uneasiness and want of confidence in things around, as if they thought themselves usurpers on the Red Indian territory. From time immemorial none of the Indians of the other tribes had ever encamped near this lake fearlessly, and, as we had now done, in the very centre of such a country; the lake and territory adjacent having been always considered to belong exclusively to the Red Indians, and to have been occupied by them.[24]

Despite failure, Cormack was not convinced the Beothuk were extinct. There were the 12 of whom Shanawdithit had spoken, and perhaps there were others. Two final expeditions were sponsored by Cormack as president of the newly founded ''Bœothick Institution'' (a concerned citizens group dedicated to ''promoting the civilization of the Red Indians of Newfoundland''). Both employed the same three Indian guides, and both ended in failure. The three guides thoroughly searched the island's interior without discovering any recent traces. When Shanawdithit died of tuberculosis in 1829, it was assumed the tribe was extinct.

At the Institution's founding assembly the myth alleging Micmac aggression took an absurd twist when Cormack, who ought to have known better, made this statement to the meeting:

> The history of the original inhabitants of Newfoundland, called by themselves Beothuck, and by Europeans, the Red Indians, can only be gleaned from tradition, and that chiefly among the Micmacs. It would appear that about a century and a half ago, this tribe was numerous and powerful—like their neighbouring tribe, the Micmacs—both tribes were then on friendly terms, and inhabited the western shores of Newfoundland, in common with the other parts of the island, as well as Labrador. A misunderstanding with the Europeans (French) who then held the sway over those parts, led, in the result, to hostilities between the two tribes; and the sequel of the tale runs as follows.
>
> The European authorities, who we may suppose were not over scrupulous in dealing out equity in those days, offered a reward for the persons or heads of certain Red Indians. Some of the Micmacs were tempted by the reward, and took off the heads of two of them. Before the heads were delivered for the award, they were by accident discovered, concealed in the canoe that was to convey them, and recognized by some of the Red Indians as the

> heads of their friends. The Red Indians gave no intimation of their discovery to the perpetrators of the unprovoked outrage, but consulted amongst themselves, and determined on having revenge. They invited the Micmacs to a great feast, and arranged their guests in such order that every Beothuck had a Micmac by his side, at a preconcerted signal each Beothuck slew his guest. They then retired quickly from those parts bordering on the Micmac country. War of course ensued.[25]

Eighteen years later the geologist J. B. Jukes repeated this story, again branding the French as the instigators:

> Their [Beothuk] destruction, however, was not wholly due to the English, the French had a still greater hatred of them, and contempt for their lives, which they even to this day preserve. Their very term "sauvages" for all whom we call Indians denotes this. The Mic-Mac Indians were, however, the most efficient instruments of their destruction.

Jukes then relates the account of the offered reward, the beheading and subsequent feast, adding with a flourish, "After this they fought at the north end of the Grand Pond, and Shannoc Brook, on the Exploits River, and, indeed, wherever they met."[26]

So it was the unscrupulous and meddling French as well as some manner of savage impulse which inspired Micmac hostility. As with Cartwright's allegation, colonial authority and society accepted the story as fact, and subsequent authors have repeated it faithfully.[27] The perpetuation of the myth is astounding, especially in light of Howley's scepticism on the matter. After citing the story by Jukes, he argues:

> The statement that the French had offered a reward for the heads of any Red Indians brought to them, is at variance with the general treatment accorded the native tribes of America by that nation, and is hard to believe. The French, it is well known, always held that the Indians were human beings, with souls to be saved, not mere animals to be destroyed.[28]

Howley's study of the Beothuk, first published in 1915, has since served as the standard reference. Nonetheless most subsequent authors have chosen to ignore his position on this issue. One of the rare exceptions is Fred Rowe:

> Here we have an example of a whole people, the Micmacs of Newfoundland (as well, of course, as the French fishermen) tarnished by charges for which, so far as I have been able to

> ascertain, there is not a scrap of documentary evidence. In fairness to all involved, critical questions should have been raised before accepting such an insubstantial rumour as historical fact.[29]

There is no supporting evidence. If such documents do exist, they would presumably be found in the French colonial records, either those of the governor in Placentia, government departments or missionary reports. Ralph Pastore has examined the Placentia material and found only one Beothuk reference "with no reference to a bounty," predictably enough, for as he notes, Beothuk territory "historically lay well to the north of Placentia."[30] Similarly, a leading authority on the history of the French fishery in Newfoundland, Charles de la Morandière, made a thorough search of the pertinent archives in France and found nothing that would suggest the French were in any way involved in the Beothuk extermination.[31]

While talk of Micmac mercenaries pursuing French bounty appears to be nonsense, how did the story originate? In his address to the Beothuk Institution, Cormack gave no indication of his source. At that point he had acquired some understanding of the Micmac people, no doubt more than others of that time, yet he never again (nor had he ever before) told the story. It appears only in this speech, unexpectedly and without apparent reason. Jukes reveals his source; the story was an "account which an old Mic-Mac Indian gave to Mr. Peyton."[32]

John Peyton immigrated to Newfoundland from England in the late 18th century and settled in the Bay of Exploits. He and his partner, Henry Miller, established a merchant business outfitting furriers and salmoniers. Peyton participated in, if indeed he did not organize, several attacks on the neighbouring Beothuk. Documents compiled in Howley's study indicate that he was directly involved in at least three punitive raids. Rowe, who otherwise defends the reputation of the settlers, frankly admits to Peyton's ruthless character:

> In 1785 Henry Miller, John Peyton Senior and Thomas Taylor, heavily armed, went up the Exploits until they came to some wigwams from which issued a number of Beothuks of both sexes and of all ages. They fired into the group, undoubtedly killing some and wounding others. The main body fled leaving a little

> girl and a crippled man who defended himself with an iron trap which Peyton wrested from him and used to beat out his brains.[33]

Reports of atrocities included several by John Bland, magistrate of Bonavista Bay. In one he states "Peyton has rendered himself infamous for his persecution of the Indians" and suggests that "to expel Mr. Peyton from the Bay of Exploits . . . would be an essential point gained in the desired end."[34]

Many of the events relating to the final days of the tribe involve the Peytons, John Senior and his son John Junior (apparently the more respectable of the two). Several captured Beothuk, including Mary March and Shanawdithit, lived in the Peyton household. Mary March was captured by the two Peytons on an expedition in 1819. Shanawdithit was held as a servant of the family for five years before moving to St. John's as a ward of the Beothuk Institution. Through these and other 'encounters' the Peytons acquired a considerable knowledge of the tribe, their lifestyle and likely whereabouts. The leaders of various expeditions—Cormack, Buchan, Glascock and others—all called on the Peytons for advice and assistance.

Imagine the incongruity of such a consultation: the infamous Beothuk killer playing host to the celebrated defenders of the tribe. Could Peyton have contrived this tale of Micmac bounty hunters to salvage something of his reputation in Newfoundland society and to absolve his guilt? More important, by circulating such a story might he have hoped to protect his family's growing commercial interests in the area? As a merchant his livelihood was directly tied to the success of the salmon fishery and fur trade pursued by the settlers he outfitted. The colonial government would have been less inclined to expel him from the area or to otherwise curtail his encroachment on tribal land had they believed that the Micmac rather than settlers posed the critical threat to the Beothuk.

Had the government acted upon their concern, if they had done other than simply issue proclamations, offer rewards, and sponsor expeditions, the outcome might have been different. The most effective measure would have legally isolated the Bay of Exploits, the river, and the adjacent interior as Indian land and strictly enforced a ban on encroachment. Such a measure was proposed by the British government in its Royal Proclamation of 1763, a statute intended to prevent further intrusion by settlers upon Indian lands on the mainland. A similar measure had been proposed in

Newfoundland. A board of inquiry at which the chief magistrate condemned Peyton also heard the testimony of Captain George Cartwright, a naval officer who was a member of his brother's expedition in 1768. Under questioning he offered a proposal:

> . . . to appropriate that part of the coast . . . to the use of the Indians, and to have some person stationed there with a schooner and a sufficient number of people to protect them. No person except those employed by his majesty to go within.[35]

Such a measure would have all but destroyed Peyton's business and, as Pastore points out, "Peyton and other northern furriers had a good deal to gain if they could link the Micmacs to the killing of Beothuks."[36] Having contrived a convenient scapegoat, they drew attention away from their own depredations and insured the continuation of their business interests. Once the Beothuk were presumed extinct, the Peytons began the construction of a sawmill in the Bay of Exploits, a venture they would not likely have considered were there still hostile Indians about.

Whatever the origins of the Micmac mercenary myth, it remains just that, a myth. In effect it offers the reassurance that early settlers of Notre Dame Bay, however despicable their actions, merely finished what others had begun. Conveniently, the myth fitted well with both Cartwright's suggestion of savage hostility and Newfoundland's historical antagonism towards the French. It was readily accepted without raising any "critical questions."

* * * * *

The true nature of Micmac and Beothuk relations remains unclear. While Cartwright's assumption cannot be taken seriously, the possibility exists that at some point, for whatever reason, the relationship was in fact hostile. The evidence is ambiguous. On the one hand a division of tribal territory and mutual avoidance certainly does not preclude the possibility of mutual antagonism; it may even imply it. On the other, there is Cormack's rather intriguing statement in the preface to his speech on the French bounty; namely, that at one time the two tribes were "on friendly terms" and inhabited certain parts of the island "in common."

The Micmac confirm Cormack's statement. John Paul of Badger told Speck that "Long ago the Micmac and the Red Indians were friendly and lived together in a village at St. George's Bay." Speck found it was "a matter of common knowledge among the older members of the Newfoundland band, that their ancestors lived in amicable contact with the Beothuk.'' According to John Paul there was a falling out between the two:

> Everything went well between the two tribes. They used to have a large canoe at the village in which the people could cross over the bay. One time during the winter a Micmac boy killed a black weasel. As it was winter-time the weasel should, of course, have been white. The occurrence was taken as an omen of misfortune, because the boy should not have killed the black weasel in the winter-time, the animal not being in its proper hue. On account of the violation of the taboo a quarrel arose between the boys who were at the time gathered near the big canoe already mentioned. The Micmac boy struck and killed a Red Indian boy and left him there. Soon the Red Indian boy was missed by his people, and after searching for several days they found his body lying near the big canoe. When they examined the wounds the Red Indians concluded that the boy had been murdered. They accused the Micmac of doing the deed, and in a few days feeling became so intense that a fight ensued in which the Red Indians were beaten and driven out. They retreated into the interior and, being separated from the outside world, drifted into barbarism and became wilder. They always shunned the Micmac, who soon after obtained firearms and, although they never persecuted the Red Indians, were thenceforth objects of terror to them. In a few generations those of the two tribes who were able to converse together died out and there was no way left for them to come together. So living in fear of each other, yet avoiding clashes, the Micmac continued to live at St. George Bay and the Red Indians kept to the interior.[37]

Speck discounted this tale as an historical account, noting that ''it bears the marks of being a secondary explanation of some historical event.''[38] Mainland Micmac and neighbouring tribes have similar stories accounting for their hostile relations with the Iroquois.[39] In the case of such a 'myth transfer,' while the particulars of the incident described are undoubtedly fictional, the story itself probably arose from an event which resulted in a separation of the tribes. Speck concluded ''the Micmac and the Red Indians were undoubtedly on friendly terms originally,'' then parted company for some unknown reason.[40]

The implication of this friendly relationship and the possibility that some cultural borrowing may have taken place during the earlier period intrigued Speck. In a comparative study of their material culture, he was able to isolate a number of features characteristic of the Newfoundland Micmac but absent among those on the mainland and among the Labrador Montagnais, features which he attributed to Beothuk influence. In discussing their footwear for example, he explains:

> The distinctive feature of both the moccasin and the boots, however, is the red stain which they receive at the hands of their makers before being considered complete. Discussion of this peculiarity with the Indians themselves brought to light the fact that they attribute the custom of dyeing these articles red to former contact with the Red Indians. Since the feature seems to be restricted to those people, I see little reason to doubt the likelihood of the connection.[41]

The most intriguing implication posed by this period of friendly contact is the possibility of intermarriage. Both Speck and Howley recorded specific instances. Howley includes a story from Silus T. Rand of Nova Scotia, a keen student of the Micmac, who had it from Nancy Jeddore, a Micmac of Hantsport. It involves three Micmac hunters who happened upon several Beothuk lodges in the interior of the island. The lodges had been abandoned recently, their occupants apparently having fled in fear. In the hope of making friends, the three trailed the fleeing party and eventually overtook a woman whose snowshoe strap had broken. At first she was frightened and retreated from the approaches of her captors:

> After a few days, however, she became pacified, and after remaining with them for two years, she had learned to speak their language, and became the wife of that one of her captors to whom she had first become reconciled. . . . Joseph Nowlan, my informant's father, saw her many a time. . . . One summer when on the Island, Nowlan boarded with the family. The woman became the mother of a number of children.[42]

According to Rand, Joseph Nowlan had "spent a good many years in Newfoundland, and also among the Esquimaux, as his daughter informs me was the case."[43] His date of birth, 1777, would suggest the incident may have occurred around the turn of the 19th century.

Speck recorded another instance of intermarriage:

> In July, 1910, I happened to talk over ethnological matters with a family of Micmac who were temporarily camped near Gloucester, Mass. The family consisted of an aged woman, her son, his wife and child. . . . On inquiring of the young man, Joe

> Toney, where he was born, he told me in Newfoundland. Then becoming more interested, I inquired if his mother was a native of Newfoundland, and he replied that she was. After a few minutes' talk with his mother, he said that she was not a true Micmac, but that her father was an *Osa'yan•a* Indian from Red Pond, Newfoundland. This naturally startled me, because it referred indirectly to the supposedly extinct Beothuk.[44]

With Toney translating, Speck recorded her history:

> Santu was born in Newfoundland near "Red Pond" (Red Indian Lake), about seventy-five years ago (dating from 1912) [1837]. Her father, "*Kop*" (name of a red root found in the lake, according to her vocabulary), was a full-blood native of a tribe which called itself *Osa'yan•a*. . . . With her father she left Newfoundland at about the age of ten, or a little less, and removed to Nova Scotia, where she passed her early womanhood. Her mother was a Micmac woman, one of the band who lived in Newfoundland. She died it seems, when Santu was quite young.[45]

After extensive interviews Speck concluded that Santu's story was reliable, there seeming "little doubt from Santu's statements that *Osa'yan•a* descendants may be found in the maritime provinces and that the tribal name itself is one of the native terms of the tribe known in history as the Beothuk."[46]

Santu's story was again confirmed when Speck questioned John Paul on the matter. He had heard of the woman and

> . . . credited the claim that her father had been a man of Red Indian blood. He stated that the thing was not only possible, but that it might well be expected to be true, considering the sedentary habits of many of the Micmac hunters and the secretiveness of the Indians concerning the Red Indians a generation or so ago through the fear of retaliation or at least molestation at the hands of the English, since such a stir had raised over them.[47]

This last statement is intriguing. In asserting the likelihood of intermarriage, Paul seems to suggest that relations between the two tribes were amicable, certainly that the Micmac no longer took care to avoid contact. Other stories recorded by Howley and Speck tell of friendly encounters.

Paul's reference to "secretiveness" may be taken to suggest a protective attitude on the part of the Micmac, a desire to protect the Beothuk from the depredations imposed by the English. The wording of the statement is a bit vague since it is not clear whether the controversy, "such a stir," refers to the actions of the furriers or the concerns of the government. Even in the latter case, though, it may be argued that the Micmac, who were undoubtedly familiar with the misfortunes of the Beothuk, were similarly mistrustful of those armed expeditions and their misguided efforts to cultivate "a friendly intercourse." Judging from the testimony of another of Speck's informants, this was the case:

> . . . his grandfather's father was employed by the English to guide them to Red Indian Lake to try to capture some Red Indians. When he found a Red Indians' camp he would tell the poor folk to run, and then he would return and tell the Englishmen that he saw some Red Indians, but that they ran off. "The Micmacs never molested the Red Indians," declared Louis John.[48]

Sylvester Joe, Cormack's guide, selected a route that led well south of Red Indian Lake where both he and Cormack knew the Beothuk were then camped. Perhaps he also acted out of mistrust of Cormack's intentions rather than a fear of the Beothuk as later writers suggest.

There are some stories suggesting there may have been bloodshed between the two tribes. Noel Matthews, a Conne River resident employed by Howley as a guide, recounted a story told by his mother and Maurice Louis, the chief:

> . . . a Micmac with his wife who coming to the shore of the Grand Lake near where the river flows out, saw a Red Indian wigwam on the opposite side. The man proposed to go across in their skin canoe and visit them, but his wife demurred, being too much afraid of them. He however, persisted in going himself. She remained behind and concealed herself in the bushes to await events. She saw him land, and also saw two Beothucks come forward and take him by the arms, and lead him up to their mamateek, into which all three entered. After a considerable time elapsed, the two Red men came forth carrying their belongings, got into their canoe and paddled away. After a long wait seeing no sign of her husband returning, she mustered up courage to venture across. Having constructed a raft she ferried herself over, but on entering the now silent mamateek, she was horrified to find the headless body of her husband stretched on the floor. The head as usual having been carried off by the Beothucks.[49]

According to Howley:

> Mathew (Mathy) Michel also confirmed Noel Matthews' story, but gave a somewhat different version of it. He says it occurred at Red Indian Lake, and that the woman did not go to the wigwam but when her husband failed to return in due time, she made her way out to Bay St. George where she informed her people of what had occurred. The Micmacs thereupon set out in a body . . . to wreak vengeance upon them.[50]

There are several accounts of Micmac aggression. One appears in an article entitled "The Indian Scrape" by R. S. Dahl which appeared in a 1914 issue of *Newfoundland Quarterly*. It concerns "Old John Mitchell, a Micmac Indian" and a trek he made from Conne River to Piper's Hole "nearly a century ago." En route, while stopping to mend his gun strap, "he heard from the marsh he had just passed a sucking sound, like a foot drawn from/out mud":

> A thrill passed though Joe (?), as he noiselessly went ahead. Over the ridge he went and then straight towards an enormous frost split rock called the Shoprock [*sic*]. Among the fragments he crouched, gun to shoulder and cheek.
>
> Minutes passed, then a head appeared over the ridge. It was motionless, the fierce eyes trying to pierce the gloom.
>
> Slowly the man emerged with long clean cut limbs, graceful as only a savage can be. The Red Indian stood, bow in hand, silhouetted, against the purple of the setting sun. The gun spit fire, its thunder roared, and after rebounding in the air, the body glided down the long sloping rock called the Indian Scrape.
>
> Now, when travellers are night-bound in that locality, they are unable to get their Micmac guides to camp near any of the above-named rocks. No matter how brightly the lightening flashes in the fall of the year, and the booming thunder fills the animals of the lonely bush with fear and heralds torrential rains, the passing Micmacs avoid any shelter the prominent rocks afford. And when they are urged to moderate their pace they point to the Indian that Joe shot, who was petrified and can now be seen transfixed to the Indian Scrape. At night, they say, he moans and sighs in misery, and if travellers were to camp near him and cause him further anger, he would turn around and hurl the fragments of the rock at them.[51]

Another Micmac alleged to have shot a Beothuk was Noel Boss. According to a neighbour of the Peyton family, a man named Gill,

"It is said of this Noel Boss, that he boasted of having killed 99 Red Indians in his time, and wished to add one more to the number so as to complete the hundred."[52] Had he been a better shot, Shanawdithit would have been one of his victims:

> According to Mr. Peyton, she [in his custody at the time] exhibited the greatest antipathy to the Micmacs, more especially towards one Noel Boss, whom she so dreaded that whenever he, or even his dog made their appearance, she would run screeching with terror and cling to Mr. P. for protection. She called this man *Mudty Noel* ("Bad Noel"). She stated that he once fired at her across the Exploits River, as she was stooping down in the act of cleaning some venison. In proof of this she exhibited the marks of gunshot wounds in her arms and legs; one slug passing through the palm of her hand. Mr. W. E. Cormack, to whom she also showed these marks, confirms this statement.[53]

Cormack confirmed no such thing. Howley includes in his book several "stray notes in Cormack's handwriting," among them the statement, "Shanawdithit received two gunshot wounds at two different times, from shots fired at the band she was with by the English people at Exploits. . . ."[54] It would seem again that Peyton was simply covering for his own brutalities.

Perhaps more believable is a story told by Noel Matthews, as recorded by Howley:

> Noel Boss, or Basque, I presume the same individual mentioned by Peyton and others, had much to do with the Red men, but he avers that it was always of a friendly nature. This Noel Boss on one occasion met two of them, a young man and a lad, crossing a marsh, with loads on their backs. He went towards them but they ran away. He also ran and finally caught up with them as they could not go fast, being burthened with their heavy loads which they would not discard. The young man could have easily outrun him, but he would not abandon the lad, who was greatly frightened. When Boss came up with them he looked the young man in the face and addressed him, but the latter only laughed and still kept on running. Boss made several attempts to get him to stop and have a palaver, but in vain, he then turned off and let them go their way. On another occasion this same man Boss with some of his own people, came out on the banks of the Exploits River and saw a Red Indian canoe on the opposite side with several people in it. The Micmacs again tried to parley with them

> across the river but the Red men apparently did not relish their company, so they paddled away up the river.[55]

It would seem from this that, despite the friendly intentions of the Micmac, the Beothuk continued to shun them, as John Paul suggests in his story on their parting of the ways and again in this story:

> My grandfather and grandmother were once coming up Exploits river in their canoe. Suddenly coming around a bend they beheld a Red Indian and his wife in a canoe coming down. When the Red Indian saw them he quickly paddled ashore and he and his wife hurried into the woods to hide, taking only his bow and arrows. The Micmac paddled alongside the empty canoe and there saw a small child lying in the bottom, but there was nothing to eat in the canoe. Then my grandfather said to his wife: ''They have nothing to eat and must be going down to the bay (Exploits bay) for fish. Let us put some of our smoked meat in their canoe.'' So he put some meat in for a present and paddled on. When they got around the point, they went ashore and walked back through the thicket to where they would see the Red Indian's canoe. They beheld the Red Indian soon come down to his canoe, look in, then beckon to his wife, who came out. Then he pointed out to her the meat in the canoe. Then he pointed to where my grandfather had gone up-river in his canoe and paddled off.[56]

Finally, members of the Conne River Band tell two stories describing friendly encounters which shed some light on the fate of the Beothuk. In 1961, authors Farley Mowat and Harold Horwood visited Conne River during their *The Boat Who Wouldn't Float* voyage. Their host, Michael John, related the following:

> My grandfather told me that one time he was hunting on the Long Harbour River, about fourteen miles up from tidewater, when he met a band of strange people who did not hunt with guns, as all the Micmacs did in those days, but who still hunted with bow and arrows.
>
> There were nine people in the band—six adults and three children. My grandfather said that he was afraid of them at first, but that they were not hostile. However, they spoke a language that he could not understand.
>
> They used birchbark canoes as we did, and they dressed partly in caribou skins, which were painted red. They cooked their meat

> by skewering it on sticks, with the sticks set into the ground and slanted inward over the fire. They boiled water in square birch-bark pots set on stones.[57]

Melvin Jeddore of Conne River was told by his grandfather Peter, Noel Jeddore's eldest son, of another encounter with the Beothuk:

> His grandfather (i.e. Peter) was out hunting one fall around Pipestone Pond when he saw a strange Indian across the barren. At first the man seemed afraid and wanted to run away, but when he made a friendly wave he turned around and came forward.

He can recall little more of the story but that Peter's grandfather helped the Beothuk repair a broken bowstring with some caribou thong.

There is little reason to doubt the reliability of these two accounts. Michael John's is especially convincing for, as Horwood notes, it includes an accurate description of Beothuk dress and cooking. Both Peter Jeddore and Michael John were born in the early 1880s. Assuming a generation span of 30 years, there being no birth records for either of their grandfathers, probably neither was born before 1820 and further that neither encounter occurred before 1840, at which point the two would be no more than teenagers. From this it would appear that Shanawdithit was not in fact the last of her people, as is commonly believed, but that some Beothuk survived beyond her death in 1829. Among them would be Santu, born in 1837.

The composition of the band encountered by Michael John's grandfather is revealing. The ratio between adults and children, two to one, is quite the reverse of that normally found in a healthy population. The distortion may be attributed to a greater death toll among the young caused by disease and starvation.

Both areas where these encounters occurred, Pipestone Pond and the Long Harbour River, lay well within Micmac tribal territory. In shifting south from their sanctuary about Red Indian Lake (rather than north as Cormack and others suspected), these surviving Beothuk were obviously not inhibited by an intense fear of the Micmac whom they knew they would encounter.

Finally, in speculating as to a possible motive for such a migration, it is perhaps instructive to note that a line running from Red Indian Lake through Pipestone Pond and on to Long Harbour

River would roughly parallel the route then taken by caribou during their fall migration.

In closing, consider Speck's summation of the issue:

> The melancholy history of their former cogeners and speculations as to their ultimate fate are subjects that appeal strongly to the Micmac. In general the idea that the Micmac-Montagnais aided in the remorseless activities against the Beothuk arouses somewhat indignant denial among them. Despite the fact that historical notices, most of which I find have been disseminated from only one or two sources, mention the Micmac among the persecutors of the Red Indians, it must be confessed that I myself am rather sceptical on the point. The Micmac sincerely profess pity for the unfortunate tribe, and commiserate their hard life in the interior, terrified as they fancy by the encroachments of people with firearms, and driven away from the benefit of intercourse with those who could have furnished them with modern utensils and religion. The Indians of Newfoundland today regard the Red Indians as a people who were doomed to their fate through an unconquerable fear of their fellow-men, Micmac as well as European.[58]

Since the above was written some 75 years ago, the contemporary Micmac have not lost touch with this conviction and its underlying tradition that they did not persecute the Beothuk. The oral traditions have been broken, and the real tragedy is that some Micmac believe their people were responsible for the extinction of the Beothuk. They have read it in history books.

NOTES

1. Howley, *The Beothucks.*
2. Speck, *Beothuk and Micmac.*
3. F. W. Rowe, *Extinction: The Beothuk of Newfoundland* (Toronto: McGraw-Hill Ryerson, 1977).
4. L. F. S. Upton, ''The Extermination of the Beothucks of Newfoundland,'' *Canadian Historical Review*, 1977, vol. LVIII, no. 2, pp. 133-153.
5. Pastore, *Newfoundland Micmacs.*
6. Upton, ''Extermination,'' p. 135.
7. Rowe, *Extinction*, pp. 147-153.
8. Upton, ''Extermination,'' p. 135.
9. Ibid., p. 135.

10. Rowe, *Extinction*, p. 136. Rowe's assertion that competition for resources underlay the settler-Beothuk conflict is endorsed by Upton in a review of the Senator's book. ''He rightly emphasized the importance of salmon and furs that gave the conflict an economic base.'' L. F. S. Upton, ''The Beothucks: Questions and Answers,'' *Acadiensis*, 1978, Spring, Vol. VII, no. 2, pp. 150-155.
11. Howley, *The Beothucks*, pp. 54-55.
12. Ibid., p. 29.
13. Ibid., p. 35.
14. Ibid., p. 35.
15. Ibid., p. 44.
16. Ibid., p. 68.
17. Ibid., p. 44.
18. Ibid., p. 45.
19. Ibid., p. 64.
20. Ibid., pp. 68-69.
21. Ibid., p. 152.
22. Ibid., p. 152.
23. Ibid., p. 192.
24. Ibid., pp. 194-195.
25. Ibid., p. 183.
26. J. B. Jukes, *Excursions in and about Newfoundland*, 2 vols. (London: John Murray, 1842), vol. II, p. 130.
27. Ibid., p. 129.
28. Howley, *The Beothucks*, p. 26.
29. Rowe, *Extinction*, p. 103.
30. Pastore, *Newfoundland Micmacs*, p. 16.
31. Ibid., p. 16.
32. Jukes, *Excursions*, vol. II, p. 129.
33. Rowe, *Extinction*, p. 143.
34. Howley, *The Beothucks*, pp. 56.
35. Ibid., pp. 52-53.
36. Pastore, *Newfoundland Micmacs*, p. 19.
37. Speck, *Beothuk and Micmac*, p. 28.
38. Ibid., p. 29.
39. Ibid., p. 29.
40. Ibid., p. 29.
41. Ibid., p. 36.

42. Howley, *The Beothucks*, p. 286.
43. Ibid., p. 284.
44. Speck, *Beothuk and Micmac*, p. 56.
45. Ibid., pp. 58-59.
46. Ibid., p. 66.
47. Ibid., p. 69.
48. Ibid., p. 54.
49. Howley, *The Beothucks*, p. 280.
50. Ibid., p. 280.
51. R. S. Dahl, "The Indian Scrape," *Newfoundland Quarterly*, 1914, Autumn, Vol XIV, no. 2, p. 32.

    As fanciful as the quote might sound, it is apparent from the ethnological detail included earlier in the story that the author was familiar with the Micmac. Speck mentions that R. S. Dahl was "a former associate of Mr. Howley, who was also deeply interested in the Beothuck," as well as the case of Santu. Speck also refers to a letter he received from Dahl "dated June 6, 1912, from Placentia Bay," including "a list of Micmac settlements and hunters which he obtained from Mr. Howley."
52. Howley, *Beothucks*, p. 181.
53. Ibid., p. 176.
54. Ibid., p. 230.
55. Ibid., pp. 279-280.
56. Speck, *Beothuk and Micmac*, pp. 51-52.
57. Harold Horwood, personal communication, 1979.
58. Speck, *Beothuk and Micmac*, p. 47.

CHAPTER 4

Cormack and Sylvester Joe — Newfoundland interior and river systems — Caribou

It is somewhat ironic that the little we know of the early 19th-century Newfoundland Micmac is from a man not particularly interested in the tribe at all. Rather it was the Beothuk who aroused his interest.

Born May 5, 1796, at St. John's and educated in Edinburgh in botany and geology, William Epps Cormack was an imaginative and restless man, an ambitious adventurer and philanthropist. Throughout his life he travelled extensively, sometimes in pursuit of academic interests, sometimes engaged in various commercial enterprises, such as mining in California, raising cattle in New Zealand, and cultivating tobacco in Australia. As a close friend wrote on his death in 1868,

> The impulse of a strong fancy made him a wanderer—the commercial man and the explorer in one. While he sought the respectable gains of commerce, he at the same time aimed at extending international knowledge, thus contributing to the welfare and happiness of man.[1]

Of Cormack's many achievements, the most ambitious were his expeditions in search of the Beothuk. It was purely a personal and philanthropic venture, unsupported by government or any private agency. For reasons that remain inexplicable, the colonial government disapproved of the effort.[2] Though he failed to locate and befriend the Beothuk, he became the first European to traverse the island and, aside from a few who ascended the Exploits, the first to survey the interior. James Howley paid tribute:

> The modern traveller must entirely fail to appreciate the toil and hardship, and the almost insurmountable difficulties Cormack had to contend with in his great undertaking. It is only those like myself, who were privileged to follow in the wake of this intrepid explorer, before the advent of the railway, who can form any idea of what he had to go through. Accompanied only by a single Micmac hunter of uncertain reliability, he braved the terrors of the vast unknown interior, which was supposed to be filled with innumerable and savage wild beasts, such as bears, wolves, etc.,

> ready to devour the foolhardy person who would venture to invade their solitude.[3]

Whatever Howley's opinion of Sylvester Joe, there can be no doubt Cormack would never have completed the expedition, perhaps never even attempted it, without the services of his Micmac guide. A member of the Conne River Band he was intimate with the central region of that "vast unknown interior." Equally important, as an able woodsman and hunter, he was capable of supporting himself and Cormack in any terrain, familiar or otherwise.

Precisely how Cormack hired Sylvester Joe is a bit of a mystery. Cormack begins his narrative of the journey with "I engaged into my service, first, a Mickmack Indian, a noted hunter from the south-west coast of the Island,"[4] but does not explain how the arrangement was made.

In early July, 1822, they made a trial excursion to build stamina and test gear, backpacking "a circuit of about one hundred and fifty miles" from the capital to Placentia and back via Trinity and Conception Bays. Thus prepared, they sailed in early September from St. John's to the head of Random Sound. Aside from clothing, they carried a supply of dried food, two pots, firearms, ammunition, fishing tackle, and a blanket each.

The first days were especially gruelling for Cormack. Heavily laden, they trekked west through thick bush and deadfalls, advancing no more than eight miles a day. While Joe seemed "perfectly at home" under the circumstances, Cormack admitted to "apprehensions and thoughts of no ordinary kind," being, as he was, "unaccustomed to the untrodden boundless wilderness." He quickly realized, "as well for self preservation as for the sake of accomplishing the object of my excursion," he would have to follow Joe's example and adopt "the self-dependent mode of life of the Indian. . . . There was no will but ours."[5]

By the 11th of September, having broken clear of dense woods, they "descended into the bosom of the interior," the broad rolling barrens north of Placentia and Fortune bays. Progress was still agonizingly slow. Their provisions were nearly exhausted, but food was abundant; trout in the brooks and ponds, ducks and geese along their shores, a profusion of berries on the hillsides, but above all, innumerable caribou browsing the barrens:

> When we met deer in a herd, we seldom failed in shooting the fattest. The venison was excellent; the fat upon the haunches of

> some of them was two inches in thickness. We shot them with ball or swan shot, according to distance.''[6]

By early October, the barrens behind them, they were again hiking the bush. Here they found the first evidence of man, two sets of footprints clearly visible upon the moss. Joe concluded that one was that of ''an Indian who had been hunting here in the preceding year, and from the point of the foot being steep that he was going, laden with furs, to the Bay of Despair.'' The other track was that of ''an Indian who had passed by this season apparently from the Bay of Despair towards Gander Bay.''[7] This was Micmac country. A few days later, camped on the shores of a small lake, they found an abandoned birchbark canoe ''brought up from the Bay of Despair.'' The lake ''known to the Mickmack Indian as Stone Pipe Lake'' was a favourite haunt renowned for its distinctive ''magnesium rocks, out of which they carve or chisel tobacco pipes.''[8]

To the south of Pipestone, down Salmon River, lay Bay d'Espoir, Joe's home. After five weeks of hard slogging over endless miles of detours they had made it roughly midway across the island. Cormack confessed he ''felt severely the effects'' of the ''continued excessive exertion.'' The Indian, perhaps puzzled by his companion's obsession with the journey, ''complained much of the never-ending toil'' and suggested they turn south to Bay d'Espoir for a sensible respite.

By late afternoon, October 11th, they had reached the shores of Crooked Lake. Their supplies again exhausted, Joe left Cormack to stalk caribou. The next morning, with Joe still gone, Cormack saw smoke rising across the lake to the west. He fired his shotgun, assuming a Beothuk would flee, while a Micmac would respond. After Joe had returned, there appeared across the lake ''a small canoe with a man seated in the stern, paddling softly towards us, with an air of serenity and independence possessed only by the Indian.''[9] Cormack was entranced:

> After a brotherly salutation with me, and the two Indians kissing each other, the hunter proved to be unable to speak English or French. They, however, soon understood one another, for the stranger, although a mountaineer from Labrador, could speak a little of the Mickmack language, his wife being a Mickmack. The mountaineer tribe belongs to Labrador, and he told us that he had come to Newfoundland, hearing that it was a better hunting country than his own, and that he was now on his way hunting

> from St. George's Bay to the Bay of Despair to spend the winter with the Indians there. He had left St. George's two months before, and expected to be at the Bay of Despair in two weeks hence.[10]

The Montagnais, James John, expressed surprise at finding a white man so far from the sea. Cormack explained, with Joe interpreting, that he had "come to see the rocks, the deer, the beavers, and the Red Indians, and to tell King George what was going on in the middle of that country."[11] John invited the pair to return to his campsite for a day's rest. Cormack readily agreed.

> His wigwam was situated in the centre of a wooded islet at which we arrived before sunset. The approach from the landing place was by a mossy carpeted avenue, formed by the trees having been cut down in that direction for firewood. The sight of a fire, not of our own kindling, of which we were to partake, seemed hospitality. It was occupied by his wife, seated on a deerskin, busy sewing together skins of the same kind to renew the outside of the canoe. . . . A large Newfoundland dog, her only companion in her husband's absence, had welcomed us at the landing-place with signs of the greatest joy. Sylvan happiness reigned here. His wigwam was of a semicircular form, covered with birch rind and dried deer skins, the fire on the fore ground outside. Abundance and neatness pervaded the encampment. On horizontal poles over the fire, hung quantities of venison stakes, being smoked dry. The hostess was cheerful, and a supper, the best the chase could furnish, was soon set before us on sheets of birch rind. They told me to "make their camp my own, and use everything in it as such." Kindness so elegantly tendered by these people of nature in their solitude, commenced to soften those feelings which had been fortified against receiving any comfort except that of my own administering. The excellence of the venison, and of the flesh of young beavers, could not be surpassed. A cake of hard deer's fat with scraps of suet, toasted brown, intermixed, was eaten with the meat; soup was the drink. Our hostess after supper sang several Indian songs at my request. They were plaintive, and sung in a high key. The song of a female and her contentment in this remote and secluded spot, exhibited the strange diversity there is in human nature. My Indian entertained them incessantly until nearly daylight with stories about what he had seen in St. John's. Our toils were for the time forgotten. . . .[12]

Cormack was impressed by his host's proficiency as a hunter and trapper. A short distance from his wigwam was a small storage shed, "in reality a well-stock butcher's stall, containing parts of some half-dozen fat deer, also the carcasses of beavers, of otters, of muskrats, and of martens, all methodically laid out," and also "a collection of skins to sell at the sea coast."[13] His possessions consisted of two guns, some ammunition, various cooking pots, an axe, an assortment of caribou skin blankets and a canoe.

Cormack pressed for information of Red Indians. John explained that Beothuk territory lay a short distance to the north, though at this time of year they would be at Red Indian Lake. With winter fast approaching, Cormack decided to make for Bay St. George. John told him the best route, making "drawings upon sheets of birch-rind of the lakes, rivers, mountains, and woods."[14]

Cormack paid tribute to James John in his journal, saying of him:

> I'm monarch of all I survey,
> My right there is none to dispute;
> From the centre all round to the sea,
> I am lord of the fowl and the brute.[15]

They struck westward through the thick forest bordering Maelpeg Lake. They were weatherbound from the 15th until the 18th, when a sudden thaw melted the snow sufficiently for them to strike camp. After eight miles, "a most laborious walk," they discovered the Indians of whom John had spoken:[16]

> The party were encamped in one large wigwam, or kind of hut. We entered with little ceremony, my Indian kissing them all—male and female. None of them could speak English, and only one of them a little French. A deerskin was spread for me to sit on, at the innermost part of the dwelling. My Indian interpreted, and introduced me in the same particulars as before. They were Mickmacks and natives of Newfoundland, and expressed themselves glad to see me in the middle of their country, as the first white man that had ever been there.[17]

These three families, thirteen people in all, had left Bay St. George earlier that summer and were now hunting caribou, trapping marten, otter and muskrat. They planned to spend the winter at White Bear Bay.

Cormack and Joe were invited to stay. Seated with his hosts Cormack was struck by Joe's manner:

> The Indian amongst his fellows is a purely self-dependent being—an innate power of self-denial raises him above dependence upon others, and keeps him beyond their interference even in distressing wants, which yields mental triumph and glory.
>
> Want implies inability in the hunter. I observed these people bestow, and my Indian receive attention, with seeming indifference. He smoked the pipe given to him with the same composure as after a feast, although starvation and unconcealable hunger were depicted on his countenance. . . .[18]

With Joe in the lead they turned south, a course Cormack disputed, suspecting his guide was intentionally staying clear of Beothuk country. On October 29th they spied smoke rising from the woods. A canoe appeared from the opposite shore, ''paddled by two pretty Indian girls.''

> I unceremoniously saluted them in the Indian manner and we accompanied them to their camp. They were a party of Mickmack Indians, encamped at this lake because deer and firewood were plentiful. One man only belonged to this encampment, and he was out hunting when we arrived. None of the party understood a word of English; my Indian however explained. They told us, to our no little mortification, that we were yet sixty miles from St. George's Harbour, or about five days walk if the weather should happen to be favourable, and that it lay in a north-west direction. . . . This small party consisted of eight individuals—one man, four women, and three children; one an infant, was strapped or laced to its cradle, and placed upright against the side of a wigwam, as any piece of domestic furniture might be. They had left St. George's Harbour three months before; since then, had been in the interior, and intended to spend the winter at Great Cod Roy River in St. George's Bay. As every hour was precious towards the final accomplishment of my object, I propose to my Indian host to accompany me to St. George's Bay; my offer was agreed to, and a stipulation made to set off in two hours. In the absence of this Indian, who told me his name was Gabriel, his family—consisting, as already observed, of females and children—were to provide for themselves. For this purpose two guns and ammunition were left with them. One of the young women was a capital shot; during our halt with them she left the camp and shot a fat deer close by. Having partaken of the best piece of venison the interior could produce, together with smoked deer's tongues, we set off. Owing

> to our enfeebled conditions, this man's vigour and strength were enviable.[19]

The miserable weather persisted, slowing progress, but with the lakes frozen, they could strike a true course for the coast. As they were crossing a pond, Cormack witnessed an incident suggestive of the Indian's independent character. Joe had broken through the ice and struggled unaided to free himself:

> While he was struggling my new friend Gabriel stood still and laughed; Joe did not look for assistance, nor did the other evince the least disposition to render any, although he was, compared with my position on the lake, near to him. Upon my remonstrating with Gabriel about his manifesting a want of feeling towards Joe, when perishing, Joe himself replied to me, "Master, it is all right; Indian rather die than live owing his life to another." The other had acted in sympathy with the self-dependent sentiment.[20]

By October 31st they had crossed both the Annieopsquotch Mountains and the two upper sources of the Exploits, Victoria Lake and Lloyd's River. According to Gabriel the large lake at the head of the latter (which Cormack named King George IV) was a transportation terminal for the Micmac of Bay St. George, the point where they "commence and terminate their water excursions from and to the west coast. They here construct their first skin canoes upon entering the interior, or leave their old ones upon setting off on foot for the sea coast."[21]

On the evening of November 1st, atop the Long Range Mountains Cormack "rejoiced to get a view of the expansive ocean." He "hailed the glance of the sea as home, and as the parent of everything dear."[22] Success was in sight:

> November 2nd. – . . . In the afternoon we reached St. George's Harbour. The first houses we reached, two in number, close to the shore, belonged to Indians. They were nailed up, the owners not having yet returned from the interior after their fall's hunting. The houses of the European residents lay on the west side of the harbour, which is here about a mile wide, and near the entrance; but a westerly gale of wind prevented any intercourse across. Having had no food for nearly two days, we ventured to break open the door of one of the houses, the captain or chief's as we understood from my last Indian, and found what we wanted—provisions and cooking utensils. The winter stock of provisions of this provident man named Emanuel Gontgont, the whole

> having been provided at the proper seasons, consisted of six barrels of pickled fish, of different kinds, viz.: young halibuts and eels, besides dried cod fish, seal oil in bladders, and two barrels of maize or Indian corn flour.
>
> November 3rd. – We were still storm-stayed in the Indian house, in the midst of plenty. . . .
>
> November 4th. – A party of Indians arrived from the interior, male and female, each carrying a load of furs. Our landlord was amongst them. Instead of appearing to notice with displeasure his door broken open and house occupied by strangers, he merely said, upon looking around and my offering an explanation, ''Suppose me here, you take all these things''. . . .[23]

Thus ended the expedition. After a few days' rest at Sandy Point the party separated. Gabriel returned to his family at Temegan Gospen, Joe wintered with tribesmen in Bay St. George and Cormack found passage back to St. John's.

* * * * *

As remarkable as it was, Cormack's achievement was doubly fruitless. Aside from his interest in philanthropy (and his failure to locate the Beothuk), Cormack was above all a keen exponent of colonial development who regretted the economic impoverishment and geographical isolation of Newfoundland. He imagined ''some future trunk road'' would follow in the wake of his trip, a development ''which should lure men inland and forge living links between the lonely dwellers''[24] of the outports. It was not to be. To Newfoundlanders, so intimately bound to the sea, his expedition seemed no more than a curious anomaly. As one historian wrote:

> It seemed to prove nothing and to lead to nothing. It was wholly unlike anything that had hitherto occurred in the colony, and the men had to think long before they could quite make out what they had learned from it. The only thing that was clear was that they had learned a very barren geographical lesson about a very barren region.[25]

There was no escaping the fundamental dichotomies between land and sea, aboriginals and Europeans. Whatever the historical and geographical significance of Cormack's venture, it had little meaning or value to a colonial society whose interests lay elsewhere. As J. D. Rogers put it, but for the Micmac presence, ''the body of Newfoundland was like an empty skin,'' a ''husk without a kernel.''[26]

Cormack's penetration of this supposedly empty shell provides a unique glimpse of the Indian world within. His brief ethnographic observations offer a refreshing counterpoint to those of others whose views were myopic and fragmented.

Cormack estimated the native population at 150, the majority Micmac together with "some of the mountaineer tribe from the Labrador, and a few of the Abenakies from Canada."[27] The accuracy of this figure is unknown, though it may be conservative judging from the number of migrants cited in the 18th century. Alternatively the recent immigrants might not have settled permanently but returned to Cape Breton. While no direct evidence exists that any Micmac were actually forced to return, the presence of naval vessels under the governor's orders might have deterred some tribesmen from remaining.

Whatever their number, they were "dispersed in bands" among six seasonal campsites: "St. George's Harbour and Great Cod Roy River on the west coast; White Bear Bay, and the Bay of Despair on the south coast; Clode Sound in Bonavista Bay on the east; Gander Bay on the north coast."[28] They were "occasionally at Bonne Bay and the Bay of Islands on the northwest coast."[29] Given their proximity to the mainland, the Bay St. George and Codroy sites were possibly the first established by those early immigrants, the ancients, while the White Bear Bay and Bay d'Espoir sites were founded sometime later. The Clode Sound and Gander Bay sites, both at one time within the Beothuk sphere, were presumably recent. Another former Beothuk site omitted by Cormack was at the mouth of the Exploits. Other sites on the northwest coast (unknown to Cormack) were probably first occupied by Montagnais from Labrador.

Cormack sheds little light on the Montagnais, aside from indicating they were second to the Micmac in population. The two seem to have freely intermingled and intermarried within Newfoundland. From Cormack there is the example of James John, a Montagnais born in Labrador who came to the island in search of better hunting grounds and subsequently married a Micmac. Well before the time of Speck's visit in 1914 the two groups had substantially merged. Of 13 men whose ancestries he determined, six were of Micmac and Montagnais blood.[30]

Cormack noted that the historic ties with the French remained an important factor in native life. As in the days of Palliser they maintained a close economic and religious association with St. Pierre. Those settled on the south coast traded both fur and caribou meat with the French colony. They were associated with the priest there "whom they consider their confessor, and endeavour to see once in two years."[31] At the same time commercial ties with local Newfoundland merchants were developing. Perhaps it was this liaison which prompted him to suggest that the Micmac "might be rendered useful if some of the leaders were noticed by the British government."[32] There is no evidence that such notice was taken. The dichotomy endured; the concerns of colonial authorities remained fixed upon the fishery.

The Micmac subsisted as hunters, as Cormack briefly describes:

> . . . they all follow the same mode of life—hunting in the interior, from the middle of summer till the beginning of winter in the single families, or in two or three families together. They go from lake to lake, hunting all over the country, around one before they proceed to the next. They paddle along the borders and the men proceed on foot up every rivulet, brook, and rill, beavers being their primary object of search, otters, martens, musk rats, and every living thing; secondly, when the lakes are connected by rivers, or when the portages between them are short, they proceed in or carry their canoes with them; otherwise they leave these, and build others on arriving at their destination. The hunting season, which is the months of September and October, being over, they repair to the sea coast with their furs, and barter them for ammunition, clothing, tea, rum, &c., and then most of them retire to spend the winter at or near the mouths of the large rivers, where eels are to be procured through the ice by spearing, endeavouring at the same time to gain access to the winter paths of the deer.[33]

Cormack confined the hunt in the interior to September and October. He provides a hint of two critical factors which affected Micmac occupation of Newfoundland's interior; namely, caribou and canoe:

> Thanks to the paddle, their topographical knowledge was a good century ahead of the Englishman's knowledge, and the paddle was an emblem of power as well as an instrument of knowledge.[34]

The aboriginal Micmac developed and refined the intricate skills involved in the construction and handling of canoes, and found Newfoundland a country ideally suited to this mode of travel. The island's interior is gently undulating and well drained by a complex of river systems. Most are easily navigable by canoe. The campsites listed by Cormack and later explorers are all located at a river mouth.[35] At Bay St. George, Cormack noted, local hunters backpacked to King George IV Lake before boarding their canoes.

Historian Rogers compared the interior river complex to a massive tree, with branches and roots fanning out over the country.[36] Its trunk, the Salmon River, thrusts north from Bay d'Espoir through a series of lakes into the heart of the central interior, ending at Wachtewbeesh or Crooked Lake. From here one can take the westerly branch, portaging to Maelpeg (the lake of many bays) on the headwaters of the Grey River. A second portage, downstream from Maelpeg to Granite Lake, connects with White Bear River and the settlement at its mouth. Leapfrogging from system to system, the Indian voyager can connect with Grandy's Brook, the upper Exploits and Bay St. George via King George IV Lake.

The eastern branch of this system leads inland from Fortune Bay along the Bay du Nord River and connects with the neighbouring watersheds. One branch follows the main river to its headwaters below Middle Ridge, from which the traveller can portage to the source of the Terra Nova River and Bonavista Bay. A second struck east from Medonnegonix through Koskaecodde and Kaegudeck lakes toward Mount Sylvester, over the divide to Eastern Maelpeg to the headwaters of Piper's Hole River and Placentia Bay.

These river systems formed a natural infrastructure, used to travel to, from, and within hunting territories. All of Cormack's campsites are mutually accessible by way of those key portages.

By Cormack's time the Micmac had slowly expanded north into Beothuk country, eventually occupying most of it. The rivers were the chief avenue of advance. Connections were made over the height of land, establishing a series of new routes terminating on the northeast coast. Gander Bay was reached by what Cormack called the "grand route" of the Micmac, one which linked Salmon River with the source of the Northwest Gander. An extension of the western branch ran to the Humber River through Sandy and Birchy lakes, then overland to Indian River and Hall's Bay. A campsite was established there sometime after Cormack's second expedition. The great Exploits system was eventually incorporated as well, complete with two new campsites, one at the junction with its tributary Badger Brook, the other on Wigwam Point at its mouth. Noel Paul's Brook, the largest tributary of the Exploits, was adopted as the best means of access from the south coast, specifically from Bay d'Espoir via the Salmon.

* * * * *

It is difficult to imagine the immense herds of caribou that roamed the interior of Newfoundland. The current scattered population is a pathetic remnant of the original strength. Since few Europeans were then familiar with the forest and barrens where they gathered, it is uncertain how many caribou there were before the slaughter began. James Howley estimated a minimum of 100,000 while J. G. Millais[37] suggested twice that number, judging from the size of the herds observed about Middle Ridge and the Gander River. A. R. Dugmore[38] thought that "Perhaps one hundred and fifty thousand altogether would be a fairly safe estimate." A resident of Burgeo placed the total at 250,000 and increasing by 10,000 annually.[39] Whatever the case, at the turn of this century Newfoundland supported an immense woodland caribou population.

> One of the most striking features of the interior are the innumerable deer paths on the savannas. They are narrow and take directions as various as the winds, giving the whole country a chequered appearance. Of the millions of acres here, there is not one spot exceeding a few superficial yards that is not bounded on all sides by deer paths.[40]

The largest herds wintered in the southern interior, grazing on moss and lichen which blanketed the barrens. In times of heavy snowfall or ice storms the caribou would move into the woods and feed on mosses that grow on trees.

Newfoundland's caribou have few natural enemies. Black bears, though numerous, seldom bother them. Lynx, which are relatively rare, kill the young. The only significant natural predator was the wolf, but wolves have been reduced to extinction by a government-sponsored bounty (designed to protect settlers' livestock, not the caribou).

> We met many thousands of the deer, all hastening to the eastward, on their periodical migration. They had been dispersed since the spring on the mountains and barren tracts in the west and north-west division of the interior, to bring forth and rear

> their young amidst the profusion of lichens and mountain herbage, and where they were comparatively with the low lands, free from the persecution of flies. When the first frosts, as now in October, nip vegetation, the deer immediately turn towards the south and east, and the first fall of snow quickens their pace in those directions, as we now met them towards the low grounds where browse is to be got and the snow not so deep over the lichens. . . . They continue to travel south-eastward until February or March by which time the returning sun has power to soften the snow and permit of their scraping it off to obtain lichens underneath. They then turn round toward the west, and in April are again on the rocky barrens and mountains where their favourite mossy food abounds the most, and where in June they bring forth their young. In October the frosty warning to travel returns.[41]

Cormack's description of the annual migration did not account for the entire caribou population, however. A substantial number, later called the "southern herd,"[42] did not engage in full migration to and from the island's western highlands and northern peninsula. They too wintered on the barrens of the southern interior but shifted marginally northward in spring, ranging through the bordering forests. While the migratory herd began a return trek sometime in October or November, the southern herd usually moved southward in September.

For the Micmac of Bay d'Espoir, White Bear Bay and Grandy's Brook, the adjacent interior offered an abundance of fresh meat for the better part of the year. Their hunt did not encroach on Beothuk territory because of the southern herd. Big game was readily available, even at the height of winter, in sharp contrast to the Micmac experience elsewhere.[43] More important, while Micmac hunting grounds outside Newfoundland were subjected to intrusion and settlement by the early 19th century, on the island tribesmen could hunt freely over a substantial area.

With firearms the Micmac could hunt efficiently. Throughout the 19th century most hunters used muzzleloaders but were not completely dependent on them. Cormack observed they retained aboriginal skills, as demonstrated by Sylvester Joe:

> We happened to see a solitary stag amusing himself by rubbing his antlers against a larch tree on a plain; my Indian, treading lightly, approached him from behind, and struck him on the head

> with his axe, but did not knock him down; he of course galloped off.[44]

As Cormack observed, "The capabilities of some of the Indians in hunting seem almost incredible to those who have not seen their powers tried."

NOTES

1. Howley, *The Beothucks*, pp. 234-236.
2. Ibid., p. 130.
3. Ibid., pp. 232-233.
4. Ibid., p. 130.
5. Ibid., pp. 135-139.
6. Ibid., p. 143.
7. Ibid., p. 145.
8. Ibid., p. 146.
9. Ibid., p. 148.
10. Ibid., p. 148.
11. Ibid., p. 148.
12. Ibid., p. 149.
13. Ibid., p. 149.
14. Ibid., p. 149.
15. Ibid., p. 150.
16. Ibid., p. 150.
17. Ibid., pp. 150-151.
18. Ibid., p. 151.
19. Ibid., p. 157.
20. Ibid., p. 157.
21. Ibid., p. 158.
22. Ibid., p. 158.
23. Ibid., p. 159.
24. Rogers, *Historical Geography*, p. 160.
25. Ibid., p. 159.
26. Ibid., pp. 159, 169.
27. Howley, *The Beothucks*, p. 151.
28. Ibid., p. 151.
29. Ibid., p. 151.
30. Speck, *Beothuk and Micmac*, pp. 132-134.
31. Howley, *The Beothucks*, p. 153.

32. Ibid., p. 152.
33. Ibid., p. 152.
34. Rogers, *Historical Geography*, p. 163.
35. This settlement pattern had always been characteristic of the Micmac. In his study of the early historical materials, Hoffman found that of some 46 summer villages, 35 were located "near the mouths of respectable rivers, while the remainder lay on favourable locations on salt water lagoons, coves, and bays." Hoffman, "Historical Ethnography," p. 131.
36. Rogers, *Historical Geography*, pp. 165-168. The description of the route is not derived solely from Cormack and Rogers, neither of whom was fully or accurately aware of its entire extent. Rogers, for example, is probably mistaken in branching the eastern route off the Salmon River to eastern Maelpeg via Newfoundland Dog Pond. The Bay du Nord River anchors the eastern branch.
37. J. G. Millais, *Newfoundland and its Untrodden Ways* (London: Longman, Green and Co., 1907), p. 333. Later explorers, sportsmen in particular, thought this to be a bit conservative. Dugmore for example, wrote that "perhaps one hundred and fifty thousand altogether would be a fairly safe estimate."
38. A. Radclyffe Dugmore, *The Romance of the Newfoundland Caribou* (London: William Heinemann, 1913).
39. Millais, *Untrodden Ways*, p. 333.
40. Howley, *The Beothucks*, pp. 140-141.
41. Ibid., pp. 155-156.
42. The existence of this herd, first suggested by the sportsman Selous in 1900, was confirmed by Millais after his own expeditions. Millais, *Untrodden Ways*, pp. 3, 4, 325, 326.
43. For example, see Hoffman, "Historical Ethnography," pp. 151, 177, 178.
44. Howley, *The Beothucks*, p. 143.

CHAPTER 5

Growth of colony and infrastructure — Explorers — Wix, Jukes and Gisborne — Carriage of winter mail — Geological surveys of Murray and Howley — Railway surveys — Sportsmen

Newfoundland finally emerged as a true colony during the 19th century. Since the time of Palliser (1764-1768), the last governor to seriously oppose settlement, the resident population had grown substantially. In 1730 less than 30 per cent of its 3500 settlers engaged in the fishery; by 1810, 90 per cent of the 24,000 residents were fishermen.

This dramatic change in the character of the fishery precipitated a corresponding change in British colonial policy. Throughout the period of the migratory fishery, naval authorities were the government; specifically, the admiral of the convoy was appointed governor, returning to England in the fall. In 1817 it was decided that a governor should stay during the winter to administer the growing civil establishment. The legal status of settlers and their right of occupation, formerly disputed by the Crown, was given official sanction in 1819 with the decision by Chief Justice Forbes in London that

> . . . on the plea of undisturbed possession, occupancy for purposes other than the fishery was legal. For the first time since 1637, Newfoundlanders could regard their own homes as private property.[1]

This change in policy culminated in the decision of the British parliament in 1824 to establish a Crown colony. A year later a council was created to advise the governor. Representative government and responsible government followed in 1832 and 1855 respectively.

The colonial government faced several fundamental problems. Transportation and communication services were primitive, confined largely to the more populated Avalon Peninsula. Far more serious was the colony's complete and utter dependence upon the fishery, an industry incapable of consistently generating significant revenues. Periodic traumatic fluctuations in the price of fish served as reminders of its inherent instability. Clearly, if the fishery was inadequate to met the needs of the populace, there had to be alternative industries.

As the government slowly developed an infrastructure, attention gradually turned to the interior. Overland telegraph lines and mail routes were established, and a railroad was built across the island. There were hopes that timber and mineral resources would be found in a wilderness so far unexplored. Beyond the area inland from the northeast coast frequented by furriers and the country observed by Cormack and others, the interior remained uncharted.

Over the century a trickle of surveyors, geologists and engineers infiltrated the interior, mapping its contours, assessing its resources, laying the groundwork for development. Like Cormack, they invariably turned to Micmac guides. The individual efforts made by these guides is inferred from journals and reports written by men preoccupied with concerns other than recording the particulars of Indian life. Knowledge of the Micmac at the turn of the 19th century is attributable to men like Cormack who were interested in the Beothuk. For the balance of the century incidental remarks and occasional references by those whose interests lay elsewhere form the basis of Micmac ethnography. The ultimate irony lies in the fact that the developments which the Micmac helped make possible would fracture their tribal unity and threaten their cultural viability.

The first substantial penetration of the interior following Cormack was church sponsored. Edward Wix, a Protestant missionary and Archdeacon of Newfoundland, undertook an extensive 'visitation' in the winter of 1835, touring isolated settlements along the south and west coasts.[2]

The first leg of his journey, St. John's to Piper's Hole, was by road and snowshoe. He hired an unnamed guide who, though not Indian, was recommended by "the fact of his having lived, some time back, four years with the Micmac Indians," an experience Wix assumed had lent him "some acquaintance with the mode of travelling in the untractable island."[3]

From Piper's Hole the party sailed to Bay d'Espoir, landing near the Indian village. Here Wix altered his plan. Rather than making the trip by boat, he chose to make for Bay St. George by land, "a journey of eight or nine days," and return by boat along the south coast. He hired a Micmac, Maurice Louis, an able woodsman who, Wix was told, "had once walked in the depth of winter, from the Exploits across the island to Gaultois in four days."[4]

Departing Friday, February 3rd, they reached the head of the bay where they spent the night with two Indian families. Wix was impressed by the piety and personality of one of them:

> . . . his ascetic acts, and acts of real humanity, had acquired for him a character of holiness, and a great influence over his tribe. He was, at this time, under a self-imposed vow, not to break silence during the Fridays of Lent: accordingly, though the arrival of strangers was, of course, most exciting, and might have been expected to throw him off his guard, he exhibited a degree of impassiveness and of nervous control (as he lay smoking his short blackened pipe, with his feet towards the central fire) which were quite wonderful.[5]

Early the next morning Wix, Louis and the Irish guide set out, accompanied by four Indians, including two women going to retrieve cached caribou a day's walk to the west:

> The Indian squaws pleased me much by their natural courtesy. Though walking above a hundred miles in Indian rackets or snow-shoes has made me now somewhat expert in the use of them, it may be imagined that I was at first, indeed I must be still, very awkward in them, by the side of an Indian. . . . Though noisy in their mirth at their own disasters, these Indians were courteous as French people could have been, in rendering me every assistance in my difficulties.[6]

After three days of good snowshoeing, they had covered a third of the distance. This was as far as they got. Under the glare of a bright sun, all succumbed to severe snow blindness. Camp-bound for two days and unable to hunt, their provisions nearly exhausted, Wix decided to abandon the journey. Their only alternative was to make for the Indian settlement at White Bear Bay. Louis did not know that country, and his reluctance to press on led Wix to suggest a curious though perceptive analogy:

> The straggling locations of these Indians along our coast, reminded me much of the separation between Abraham and Lot. The reasons, in the case of the Indians, who separate son from father, and brother from brother, that they may have uninterrupted space for their hunting and furring excursions, are similar to those which led the patriarchs to live apart, that they might have ample space for their pastoral pursuits.[7]

In an effort to discover the resources of the interior, the colonial government sponsored a geological survey in 1839. J. B. Jukes, an

English geologist engaged for two field seasons, reported three meetings with Micmac. In August he ascended the Humber River by schooner and dory, observing a single settler family on one shore of Humber Sound, and opposite them, "an Indian wigwam, with an old Indian woman and her two daughters":

> The old woman had a kind of moustache tattooed on each cheek, and spoke nothing but Indian, but one of the daughters could speak English. They were busy making baskets and moccasins, and were very neat, tidy, civil people. I bought a pair of very pretty moccasins for half a dollar, made of dressed deer-skin (like Woodstock gloves), and ornamented in front with bits of coloured cloth. The wigwam was composed of a frame of poles like that before mentioned, and covered with large strips of birch bark, kept in their place by other poles resting upon them. The top of the cone was left uncovered to let out the smoke, and the door was closed by a curtain of deer-skin. There was a small fire on the ground in the centre, around which was arranged a layer of small boughs and twigs of fir in a circular fan shape, forming a mat to sit down on. They sat something like the Turks, with their legs doubled under them. An Indian man, the husband of one of the daughters, was living with them, but was now away in the woods.[8]

After leaving the Humber, Jukes headed south around the Port au Port Peninsula into Bay St. George, where he heard rumours of an inland coal deposit located by a large lake.

Landing August 25th at Sandy Point, a community "about half French and the rest English, Jerseymen, and a few Indians," Jukes "strolled about the neighbourhood to make acquaintance with the people, and get intelligence of the interior of the country" and

> met with an Indian at one of the wigwams, named Sulleon, a very decent fellow, with a good character. He told me that he had a boat on the great pond I had heard of, and that the nearest point of it was within twenty miles of the harbour, and that he knew all the country perfectly well. He said it would take a week to go and come back again, and he agreed to go with me as a guide, taking my four men to carry provisions.[9]

Grand Lake, Jukes' objective, was Sulleon's hunting ground. On its shores he had several wigwams and a boat, all at the surveyor's disposal. At dawn on the 29th the party set off, taking with them "a small sprit-sail for Sulleon's boat" and various supplies, while the Indian packed "a bundle of his own things he was taking in for his family, as he intended to live at the pond during the winter.''[10] For two days they hiked along ''a little path heading through the woods, which none but an Indian would have found'' and over a ''rough, uneven, scrubby, yet soft and wet spongy mass of moss. . . .''[11] Exhausted by Sulleon's pace, Jukes could not help envy how

> the Indian got on most easily, with his toes turned in, his back bent, and a light yet slouching kind of gait, dexterously avoiding the high knobs and the deep holes, and keeping a steady pace over all impediments.[12]

Finally, at Grand Lake Sulleon led the party down a brook to his wigwam on the lakeshore, where they pitched camp.

That evening, out after black ducks, Jukes was treated to a demonstration of 'tolling':

> Sulleon saw one of these ducks on the wing a long way off, and, pulling me down with him into some bushes, he pinched his nose with his finger and thumb, and then quacked so naturally that the bird flew right over us, and I shot him as he passed.[13]

It was another Indian, one of Sulleon's friends, who discovered a three-foot seam of coal three years earlier. Boat and sail prepared, the party set off, for two days running a strong southwest wind. This was deep water and treacherous sailing, Jukes discovered, but Sulleon proved an able seaman:

> That the water is of great depth is certain, for as we drifted before the blast great rolling waves followed us, higher than our heads, and even calming occasionally the lower part of the sail. This, although only a small sprit-sail, we were shortly obliged to reef, leaving a triangle not much bigger than a pocket-handkerchief; and even then the one man sat with his foot against the step of the mast, while another supported it from behind to prevent its being blown out. Sulleon steered with a paddle, and it was entirely by his skill that we were two or three times saved from being swamped by the great rollers that swept after us.[14]

On September 1st they landed near the outflow of Sandy Lake. Jukes examined the coal seam, finding it smaller than expected but of good quality. He reconnoitred the tableland above the lake, and looking west, could see the lower Humber. To the north were visible ''two or three low blue hills . . . which Sulleon said were close to the head of White Bay.''[15]

The party returned, this time passing west of Glover Island, keeping a sharp lookout for caribou. Stormbound the next day, Sulleon landed them on the island where he expected better luck. Their supplies were running critically short:

> Leaving two men with the boat, the two others, Sulleon, and myself, set off with our guns. After a stiff and toilsome climb up the woody precipice we arrived at some open marshes at the top, sloping gently towards the centre of the island, where were several ponds, one about three miles long. There were plenty of deer-tracks, but no deer visible. . . . We then separated; Sulleon went down to the pond, while I went up to some rocky eminences to try to find some ptarmigan, the utter absence of which rather surprised us. After hunting some time in vain, I heard a shot, and shortly after another. Running was out of the question, but I made what haste I could across the marsh to the knoll where I had left the two men stationed with my rifle. They had heard no shot, but on looking about we saw Sulleon sitting on a rock about half a mile off, and on our coming up to him he said, with all the unconcern in the world, ''I hab killed a fat buck.'' Following him down through a thicket into a little marsh, we found the fellow lying on his back, a great beast as big as a small heifer, and shot right through the heart. Sulleon had seen him swim across the pond in the centre of the island, watched where he landed, and stole down through the tangled woods, as none but an Indian can steal, till he came within thirty yards of the beast without disturbing him. We shortly had him skinned, disembowelled, cleaned, and cut up. Sulleon being used to it doubled up one side for his load, which could not be less than a hundred-weight, my two men took a quarter each, while I made a bundle of the lower jaw with the tongue, the heart, the liver, and a good portion of the tripe, etc., selected by Sulleon, and used by him for different purposes, all wrapped up in the skin.[16]

Jukes was impressed by his guide's ability to stalk prey. Sulleon explained that he more commonly hunted caribou ''by watching them swim across the lake at particular points, and then chasing them in his canoe and stabbing them in the water with a short iron spear.''[17] Such a method saved ammunition and involved less work, towing the animal by boat rather than backpacking it through the bush.

The next day after several hours' rowing, Sulleon landed the party at another campsite intending to leave a portion of the kill for winter grub. He ''proceeded to cut some of the meat into long strips, which he hung up in the wigwam on sticks over the fire,'' curing the flesh and thus preserving it for use later in the season, a cache for his family when they returned.[18] He explained that it was common for his people to ''dry the venison in this way . . . and then use it without cooking, carrying it with them on their hunting expeditions.''[19]

The meat cured and cached, the party sailed another day to the southwest end of the lake, then overland to Bay St. George, arriving September 6th. Jukes remained there a couple of days composing a report. The expedition with Sulleon was Jukes' most adventurous inland journey.

After sailing around Cape Ray to the Great Codroy River, Jukes visited several wigwams near the river mouth and talked with the occupants:

> This young Indian was about thirty, a fine intelligent fellow, with a noble countenance and piercing black eye. About two years ago he had fallen, while carrying a barrel of flour, and his back was so severely injured that he has not been able since to walk without crutches. His wife was an exceedingly pretty woman, with a Grecian countenance, dark but ruddy complexion, and a sweet smile. She spoke no English, and was very modest and reserved. They had been married ten years and had three children. Her husband gave me much information as to the interior of the country. . . .[20]

Jukes had come to Codroy in search of another deposit of coal discovered by Indians. On this occasion his inquiries met with polite but firm resistance; the area in question they intended to protect as their own, as Indian territory:

> One Indian woman, middle-aged, and apparently intelligent, began talking about the ''Indian king.'' She said that they had a ''king,'' who resided in Nova Scotia, that the whole country rightly belonged to him, and that he must be consulted before any of them dare give me any information.[21]

Knowing of the alienation of Micmac lands on Cape Breton, these tribesmen wished to avoid similar developments within their hunting grounds, hoping to warn Jukes off with references to the ''Indian king,'' the Grand Chief of the Micmac. The man who discovered the coal, Maurice Lewis, an immigrant from Cape Breton who arrived in 1815, would later be appointed Chief of the Newfoundland Micmac by the Grand Chief.

Unoffended by this rebuff, Jukes wrote appreciatively (though perhaps a little patronizingly):

> The Mic Mac Indians inhabiting Newfoundland reside chiefly on its western side, wandering from Fortune Bay to St. George's, and thence to White Bay and the Bay of Exploits, living in the winter on the products of the chase, and in the summer joining in the fishery, or getting other desultory employment. Their number probably does not exceed a hundred families, and they bear on the whole a good character. A few of them are worthless vagabonds, and, especially when intoxicated, are not to be depended on; but the greater number are honest, well-meaning fellows, and when well treated are faithful and steadfast. Sulleon and the cripple at Codwy River were men of a superior stamp, both morally and intellectually; and had the latter been well and unhurt, I would rather have had them for companions in the interior than any of the Europeans I met on the coast. They are all Roman Catholics; and Sulleon's daughter having been recently married to a young Indian when I was in St. George's, they had gone across the country to White Bay, a short time before our expedition, to have the ceremony performed by a Roman Catholic priest, who, they heard, was travelling upon the north coast of the island. . . . From all I could hear they are a very moral people, being especially strict with regard to their women and marrying at a very early age.[22]

Jukes' second field season was confined to inspecting coastal topography and one limited foray up the Exploits River. This area had already been explored, the resident Peytons providing assistance. It was here that Jukes heard the story of Micmac mercenaries and French bounty.

Without funds for additional work, the geological surveyor became a "non-entity." He conveyed his pessimism on the prospects of mineral development: "In the interior of the country, search for such uncertain things would be endless and should they exist, their discovery must be left to chance."[23] Jukes submitted a recommendation for future work, citing the Micmac as essential to success. The Terra Nova River he felt was the best point of departure:

> by getting a good Indian as a guide, excursions might be made out to Bay d'Espoir on one side, Gander Bay on the other . . . but it would require a good party and preparations, and, above all, a Micmac Indian or two.[24]

* * * * *

In 1850 the government passed "An act for the appointment of Electric Telegraph Commissioners and for incorporating Electric Telegraph Companies."[25] The commissioners were to assess the feasibility of a telegraph line from St. John's to Port aux Basques to connect with a proposed submarine cable across Cabot Strait. They approached "a gentleman of much experience in the establishment of Electric Telegraphs in British North America," F. N. Gisborne, negotiating a contract "for the arduous and important duty of making an exploratory survey of that part of the Island over which the line would pass."[26]

The coast between Fortune Bay and Port aux Basques, wild and inaccessible, indented by steep fiords, was sparsely populated. Though the shoreline had been surveyed, the adjacent interior had not.

On September 17th, 1851, Gisborne's party arrived at Piper's Hole via Chapel Arm. From there the survey party advanced, charting the course; a support team cached provisions at the head of bays intersecting the route. The survey party advanced, leapfrogging from bay to bay, Long Harbour, Conne Arm, Bay de Nord, White Bear Bay among them, arriving at Port aux Basques on November 13th.[27]

The party included five Indian guides—Joseph Paul, John Brazil, Benjamin, Frank Paul and M. Brazil.[28] Whether Gisborne hired them in the field as needed or whether he made advance arrangements, he was aware of Micmac presence and their skills. The Brazils were likely hired at Conne River, where Gisborne arrived October 18th. The Pauls, then at Grandy's Brook, knew the country between White Bear Bay and Port aux Basques. On the last leg of the survey, with winter closing fast, Gisborne relied solely on the aid of the Indians "in lieu of my St. John's men." He later reported:

> From White Bear Bay I departed on the 31st October, in company with two Indians only, and arrived at the bottom of La Poile Bay on the 7th November, and thence via Gavio to Burnt Island Brook, at which point I was effectually prevented from proceeding by a heavy and continuous fall of snow, which was soon two feet deep upon the barrens, and drifted to the extent of 6, and even 10 feet deep in the gulshes. On the 13th ult., therefore, (Cape Ray being in full view) and Port-au-Basques being but one

> days walk in advance of us, we were obliged to turn our steps seaward in search of a long point of the land upon which a few fishermen were known by the Indians to reside.[29]

These Indians were Joseph and Frank Paul. Gisborne refers to a deposit of silver ''found by the Indians in the country''[30] but said little else.

He presented ''a chart shewing the courses of the proposed line of Telegraph, accompanied by an estimate of the cost of building it.''[31] The commissioners in turn recommended to Governor Sir John LeMarchant that construction begin. Work crews erected poles and strung the line, building repeater stations at the heads of bays. In 1856 the line was completed, the submarine cable to Cape Breton was laid, and Newfoundland was part of an international communications system.

To maintain the line required repair crews at the repeater stations. The line was vulnerable to damage. Especially destructive were 'glitter' or ice storms, the weight of the built-up ice snapping wires and poles. A later writer describes the repair procedure:

> When a break occurred east or west of the station a man would be sent out with three dogs harnessed to a train. On the sled he would carry his repair kit, food, insulators, a coil of wire, snowshoes, blankets and the indispensable gun without which he never travelled. Wolves were then still prevalent in Newfoundland at that time, hunting as usual in packs, and they were an ever-present menace when hungry. The circuit covered by a linesman was usually from 30 to 50 miles. Often he had to contend with blizzards and sleet storms. . . . Sometimes he was half-starved when his food ran out from some delay experienced along the way.[32]

The telegraph company hired Micmac repair crews. None were better qualified, nor as familiar with the country. Men of the John family then living in Fortune Bay maintained the line from Long Harbour to Piper's Hole. The Benoits in Bay de Nord worked the section between there and White Bear Bay. Families at White Bear Bay and Grandy's Brook, were also engaged as repairmen.

* * * * *

Throughout the first half of the 19th century mail delivery was handled by a government packet service, with vessels assigned a particular stretch of coast. Ice left many settlements ''cut off from all communication'' over the better part of the winter. An overland route was proposed. Under the direction of Postmaster General John Delaney, Smith McKay was contracted in 1863 to map a land route from the Isthmus of Avalon to Greenspond and Twillingate.[33]

Departing St. John's on March 3rd, McKay went to Sound Island, Placentia Bay, where he met three Micmac from Piper's Hole. Each had a dog sled and provisions to which McKay added his outfit and 60 pounds of mail. On March 17th they started inland, following the telegraph line, then due north over open country, past the Dirty Scrape, across Terra Nova, on to Gambo Pond and Freshwater Bay:

> We crossed Fresh Water Bay, about 2 miles to Mrs. Prichard's where I put up for the night. From this point I dispatched one of the Indians to Greenspond with the mails, he taking the ice here. I wrote the Postmaster, that he could detain him two days, and then dispatch him with return mail, addressed to the care of Mr. Phillip Brown, Sound Island, having left instructions with him to forward this mail by the Placentia Packet, provided she reached there previous to my return. (I may here add, that this Indian returned and delivered the mail to Mr. Brown on the 4th of April, and he, (Mr. Brown) dispatched it by the Placentia Packet on the 20th. . . .)[34]

McKay and the two remaining Micmac again struck inland, bearing northwest for Gander Bay, Twillingate Island, and finally Exploits Island, making deliveries and picking up return mail. From Exploits they returned to Sound Island via the Northwest Gander. Arriving April 20th after five weeks' travel, they had covered 350 miles. McKay was the first recorded European to traverse the main body of the island, north to south.

McKay recommended the route from Piper's Hole to Twillingate via Freshwater and Gander bays. Subsidiary lines could serve Trinity and Bonavista bays:

> The orange lane, as laid down upon the accompanying map, is intended to represent the winter route, crossing the ponds and lakes at the most convenient places; by a little deviation, a good summer line could be opened, avoiding all the ponds, and but one river Terra-Nova Pond River to cross; however, there is abundance of good timber on the brook suitable for bridges. From Freshwater Bay to Gander Bay, the distance, in a direct line, will not be much over thirty miles. I understand from Charles Francis, an intelligent Indian living at the latter place,

> that the country is very level, and free from ponds and large brooks.[35]

Delaney considered McKay's proposal impractical, being "too far in the country for any useful purpose beyond that of a mere Indian track."[36] He commissioned another survey for a route closer to the coast. In the meantime, he noted, "It would be desirable to employ the Indians in conveying the mails the ensuing winter."[37] Delaney's 1864 annual report stated that "a contract was made with two Indians last winter to convey the Mails (four trips) overland, from Brigus to Fogo and Twillingate."[38] Louis John of Conne River covered the route from Brigus to Greenspond, while Charles Francis of Gander Bay did the remainder.[39]

The success of the Northern Mail Route depended on native couriers. As Delaney noted, "It will, indeed, I fear, be a difficult matter to get the latter service performed by residents without any clearly defined route" and with "no settlements or tilts on the route to afford accommodation or shelter."[40]

Another route was later established. In 1876 the postmaster general reported:

> It has been suggested that it would be of much importance to the Northern Districts and also to St. John's, if mail for the District of Twillingate and Fogo were forwarded by the S. S. *Tiger* on her next trip West, to be dispatched from Harbour Briton via Conn River, for Exploits, &c. The messengers on their return would probably bring the very earliest intelligence of the Seal Fishery, which will be looked for with much interest. A similar Service was performed last year; I therefore beg leave to recommend it.[41]

Mails for northern settlements were conveyed from the south coast by two overland routes. The first, inland from Piper's Hole in Placentia Bay, served the coast from Trinity Bay to Twillingate Island. The second, connecting Conne River with the Exploits and Hall's Bay, was pioneered by the Stephensons of Hall's Bay and the Johns of Conne River.

* * * * *

Newfoundland geological surveys resumed in 1864 with Alexander Murray. Murray—later assisted, then succeeded by James P. Howley—undertook extensive surveys, mapping geological structures and scouting commercial resources. Between 1870 and 1876,

Murray and Howley launched five expeditions, all with Micmac guides.[42]

Their reports detail their approach to interior exploration. Following Jukes' suggestion, they travelled the interior by canoe. Rogers notes that they "adhered to the better plan, which is the Indian plan, of moving on the wet instead of on the dry, and of following watercourses instead of watersheds."[43]

On his first major inland expedition, Murray departed Bay d'Espoir to ascend the Salmon River, planning to portage to a northerly-flowing river to traverse the island. He hired "four Indians from Conne River, procured canoes" and awaited a break in the season.[44] Through various delays it was too late to "effect more than a preliminary survey."[45] Intent on completing the work, he cached camping gear with a Gaultois merchant and his canoes were "left for repair (which they much needed) with the Indians."[46] In 1870 the survey was completed; Murray, an assistant and five Indians aboard three canoes paddled the Salmon River system between Long Pond and Island Pond. Low water levels forced Murray to abandon the planned portage.

The following year Murray ascended the Exploits River with "a party of Indians"[47] to Red Indian Lake. In 1874 he surveyed the Gander River below Gander Lake with the help of "Charles Francis, the Indian guide."[48]

James Howley made his first expedition inland in 1875, completing a traverse of the island from north to south via the Exploits River. Murray rendezvoused with "a crew of three Indians"[49] in St. John's before sailing to the Bay of Exploits where he:

> . . . expected to meet two more Indians who engaged to cross over by land to meet him from Bay d'Espoir, but they failing to arrive, he was compelled to engage two others, residents at Wigwam or Upper Sandy Point, to convey his stores and camp equipment up the river. The Bay d'Espoir men, however, arrived shortly after he had left, and overtook him at Badger Brook, about 35 miles up the stream, and thus his party was completed.[50]

After three months in the field they had covered the Lloyd's and Victoria rivers and twice descended to the coast, breaking out at La Poile and White Bear Bay.

Howley extended Murray's investigation of the Gander system. Murray's letter of instruction to Howley contains a warning:

> As early as possible in June, my desire is that you proceed to the Gander country, to survey as far as you can the upper branches of that river beyond the great lake. I have already written to Mr. Peyton, of Twillingate, to engage the services of Charles Francis (Indian), to accompany you; but I told Mr. Peyton, at the same time, that there had been some serious complaints made against Francis to the Government, which, unless he could clear himself of, I might scarcely be justified in giving him employment. This matter you can investigate on the spot. For my own part, I believe he is more "sinned against than sinning." If you can get another Indian from Conne to cross over and join you on the Gander (Peter Stride, for example), do so, and I think, of course, you will have John Stephenson. . . .[51]

In any event, as Howley later reported, he left St. John's "accompanied by one Indian" for Gander Bay where he was "joined by two more Indians from Bay D'Espoir."[52] They surveyed the Northwest and Southwest Gander rivers, ending with a portage from the Gander Lake to Middle Brook, and Freshwater Bay.

* * * * *

A Newfoundland railway survey was the idea of Sandford Fleming, later of CPR fame. In 1868, he financed an exploratory survey to assess the feasibility of a Newfoundland track.[53]

Talk of a railway quickly captured the imagination of island politicians and citizens. In 1875 Reverend Michael Morris addressed a large public meeting in St. John's, calling on Newfoundlanders to seriously consider "this grave and pregnant topic." He described a railway as an "engine of commerce and civilization" whose construction would lay open the undreamed of resources of the interior. Citing the work of Alexander Murray, an advocate of the railway, he talked of "the valuable forests now worthless and fallow, [the] manifold indications of coal, of magnetic iron, gypsum and china-clay."[54]

Thus prompted, the legislature acted later that year, approving funds for a preliminary survey to determine the most direct and practical route to link the capital with the west coast. Three survey teams including support crews of packers and axemen were hired. Each was assigned particular sections of the route; each included Micmac guides. Party A surveyed eastward from Bay St. George over the Long Range and Annieopsquotch Mountains to Lloyd's River. Two Micmac, Stephen Jeddore and Frank Bernard, joined them en route.[55] Party B included five Micmac: Peter John, Noel Bernard, Joseph Bernard, Noel Louis Senior and Noel Louis Junior. After ascending the Exploits and Lloyd's rivers by canoe to Party A's terminal, this crew extended the line east to the Northwest Gander.[56] The final leg of the route, covered by Party C and two Micmac, Edward Pullet and John Barrington, led west from Piper's Hole over Middle Ridge to Gander River.[57]

The survey, completed over the summer of 1875, was the most substantial assault yet on the interior; three crews, almost 100 men in all, and three months' labour. While the surveyors, mostly Canadians, were veterans of bush work, the Newfoundlanders employed on support crews had little experience. The surveyors complained of slow progress. Party B abandoned one of its canoes after it had been "rendered totally useless" by the "non-intelligence of the persons conducting it."[58] In Party C a "spirit of discontent" erupted. One of the Micmac guides "fostered their fears of the unknown country by [telling] stories of the dangers and difficulties there existing."[59]

The Micmac provided indispensable support as couriers, travelling to the nearest telegraph station with progress reports and requests for supplies. They escorted men who were injured or ill to the nearest settlement. They advised the surveyors on local weather conditions.

The line was never built, which was fortunate for the Micmac, as such a route would have sliced through the very heart of their hunting grounds.

* * * * *

At the turn of this century the Micmac played host to an entirely different sort of stranger on the country, the sportsman. These were gentlemen hunters, affluent Englishmen and Americans, veterans of expeditions to Africa, Asia and North America, who thrived on the challenge of wilderness hunting. They came in pursuit of trophy stag caribou. Over the years Newfoundland acquired a considerable reputation as a sportsman's paradise. Cormack described abundant wildlife, recommending that, "No country in the world can afford finer sport than the interior of this island."[60]

Captain W. R. Kennedy, commander of H.M.S. *Druid*, acknowledged as the "best all-round sportsman in the Royal Navy" (as well as "one of the most humorous after dinner speakers in England")[61] led several hunts. While anchored in Hall's Bay, he approached two Micmac hunters from the small encampment there and requested a canoe trip into the interior for caribou. Following the route Sulleon had described to Jukes (ascending Indian River and portaging to Sheffield Lake) the party reached Grand Lake, where they met a group of Micmac just "returned from their traplines":

> We found them most comfortably established in a wigwam, beautifully constructed to keep out the wet. They said they had done pretty well with beavers, and the interior of the wigwam was festooned with skins, stretched out to dry.[62]

Two Micmac agreed to guide Kennedy onto the barrens. One of them, "a tall powerful fellow, Levi by name, led the way up the slopes, playfully wielding an axe to clear away any obstacles on the path, and carrying a load of 100 lb. on his back."[63] Kennedy was delighted when told "not a white man had ever trod those barrens before."[64] Of the Micmac he wrote:

> These people emigrated originally from Nova Scotia; they lead a happy life, and in some respects are more independent and better off than their white brethren, whom they hold in supreme contempt. They are far better hunters and trappers, and are not to be excelled at lumbering, boatbuilding, polling up rivers, and all the incidents of a backwoodsman's craft. They know every inch of the country, and follow a trail with the sagacity of an animal. As a rule, they are sober and honest, although they have the credit of being exactly the reverse. The Indian leaves his home in the early spring, and takes to the woods in quest of beavers, otters, foxes, and martin-cats; of these the beaver is the most valuable, the fur of a full-grown beaver fetching as much as sixteen shillings, more or less, according to the quality. . . . Having obtained all the skins he can pack either on his back or in his canoe, the Indian, as the winter draws near, establishes himself on the banks of a lake, where the dear [*sic*] are in the habit of crossing in their annual migrations from north to south; he then kills what he wants for his winter supply of meat, and makes tracks for home, where he disposes of his furs in exchange for pork, flour, tea, molasses, tobacco, and such like necessaries of life.[65]

J. G. Millais, an English naturalist and explorer, planned to further his study of natural history in Newfoundland. As important to him as a trophy stag was his desire to explore new country and observe wildlife. Newfoundland offered an ideal challenge:

> It may seem strange to the reader that there should still be unexplored districts in a small island like Newfoundland which has so long been a British colony, and yet it is a fact that out of a total area of 42,000 square miles, at least two-thirds of the country is still as little known as it was when John Cabot landed.[66]

Between 1902 and 1906 Millais made four expeditions. The first two were launched from the north, ascending the Terra Nova and Northwest Gander Rivers with the aid of two settlers. The results were satisfying enough, several respectable stags, but like another sportsman, F. C. Selous, who preceded him up Terra Nova River a few years earlier, Millais was convinced that the southern area would offer better hunting. Moreover some of that interior had yet to be explored. His third venture was on the Salmon River. In September, 1903, he hired Joe Jeddore, a Micmac from Conne River, as guide. Millais' intention was to attempt the same traverse as Murray had planned in 1870, portaging from the upper Salmon to one of the northerly flowing rivers.

Supplies and canoes were backpacked from Conne River overland to Long Pond:

> Long Pond is a dangerous lake to cross. Being high and open, the wind rises rapidly, and a slight breeze will create such a "jabble" on the lee shore that canoeing must be undertaken with caution. Two years previously Joe had nearly lost his life in this lake. He was accompanying a white man on a short hunting trip, and on his return the lake "looked" easy to pass. To Joe's experienced eye, however, things seemed otherwise, and he advised waiting a day till it was calm. His master, however, was in a hurry, and decided to chance it, with the result that both boats were flooded as they approached the southern shore, and sank in about five feet of water. If the accident had occurred two minutes earlier, all on board must have been drowned.
>
> Next day, accordingly, Joe shook his head when he spied little white waves breaking on the distant shore, so we remained till midday, afterwards making a start up the shore to the narrowest crossing place, about a mile and a half wide, and the wind being slight, we paddled across in none too pleasant a sea.[67]

Millais acquired an appreciation of Joe Jeddore who exhibited natural ability as a canoeist:

> Standing up in his boat, he poled it through rapids and past rocks in a way that excited our wonder and admiration. The less skilled white men were in the water all the time, hauling, guiding and lifting, and Little Bob distinguished himself by falling out of his boat into the river. Consequently Joe was always about half a mile ahead of his companions, for whom he waited with a sort of patronising air.[68]

At Round Pond, Millais struck east through Newfoundland Dog Pond by portage to the Northwest Gander River. This was Cormack's "grand route" of the Micmac. This was relatively new country to Jeddore; however, Joe's father Nicholas had guided "a miner named Guzman"[69] over the area in 1875. Joe Jeddore proved the complete guide:

> . . . he made it his business to go and find out the condition of the brook and its fitness or otherwise for canoes. He said nothing to me, but at four the next morning I detected him lighting his pipe by the fire. He slipped silently past my bed and, making his way to a canoe, paddled away swiftly into the darkness. At half-past eight Joe was sitting at breakfast with the others. He had run six miles up the river and back, twelve miles in all, and knew all about the stream. I liked that, because it showed a strict attention to business and proved that he had our interests at heart.[70]

In the family hunting territory of Noel Matthews and his sons, Martin and Michael, of Conne River, Millais asked their assistance on the portage. "This they agreed to do, and so met us on the following morning by the brook side, where they at once took pack to help lighten the canoes."[71] Within a few days they completed the portage to the upper reaches of the Gander beneath Burnt Hill; Millais was the first to map its contours. After photographing his 'discovery' he hunted on the Gander, while the others in the party followed, packing gear. With Jeddore's help in spotting and stalking prey, Millais made nine kills including "three fine specimens," before arriving at Gander Lake and the railroad town of Glenwood.[72] Here the expedition ended.

Millais concluded that part of the southern herd summered between the Gander and Terra Nova Rivers and migrated south along trails converging near of Mount Sylvester.[73] There, on the barrens above Fortune Bay, he expected fine hunting. The Long

Harbour River, as yet unexplored, would provide access. Millais contacted Joe Jeddore, but he had:

> . . . made other plans to go trapping with his brother Nicholas. Nevertheless, he was good enough to delay his trip for several days, to make sure that I could obtain the services of one Steve Bernard, who alone knew part of the Sylvester country, and another excellent Indian, John Hinx, whose hunting-ground lay to the east in the neighbourhood of the Eastern Maelpeg.[74]

Arriving September 30th, 1906, Millais was met by Phillip Ryan, the Long Harbour telegraph operator, and two Micmac from Conne River, Micky John and Paddy Hinx. "They told us that Steve Bernard and John Hinx were both on their way, the former from Bay Despair, and the latter from his 'tilt' up to the north east, to meet me."[75] They advised against ascending the river without help.

> This was rather serious news, as I had hoped to do my trip with two Indians; however, the difficulty was solved by the arrival on the following day of Matty Burke and Johnny Benoit, who agreed to come with me for seven days, and to help Bernard and Hinx with the boats until the worst of the rapids were passed.[76]

With their arrival, the party set out:

> Matty Burke is a half-bred Frenchman of about thirty-three. In the river he was invaluable, and very skilful with the pole. Ashore he was a splendid camp man, being a good cook and excellent woodman, as all the Indians are. In appearance he was a picturesque ruffian of the old *coureur-de-bois* type, and would have made an excellent stage villain at the Adelphi. At first he seemed to be of a somewhat suspicious nature, and was always watching me out of the corners of his eyes, but this soon wore off, and he became the gayest of the party when his buoyant Gallic nature asserted itself.[77]

> Johnny Benoit was of quite a different type, a visionary boy of eighteen, with great, big, dreamy black eyes. He had the sort of expression that sees "God in clouds, and hears Him in the wind." He was very good-looking, but did not like work, partly because one of his arms was half paralysed through rolling logs when he was too young, and partly because he had fallen over a precipice two years previously and been half-killed. But he was a nice, amiable creature, and with his dislike for labour, quaint thoughts, and sweet far-away expression, would have made a successful minor poet at home.[78]

Steve Bernard was "twenty-eight years old, strong as a bull, and good-natured to the highest degree":

> When he was not singing mournful Indian dirges and Gregorian chants, he was generally laughing or chaffing John Hinx or the others, and I found him an excellent guide and hunter in his own province. Like all the Indians he loved deer hunting, and soon became proficient with the telescope. His capacity for carrying heavy weights was extraordinary. "I like to take those," he said one day, making a grab at my coat, rifle, telescope and camera, which I had set aside for my own small pack, when crossing a mountain range, and flinging them on the top of his hundred-pound pack, "and when we come to the brook, you climb on top, sir." This I did by way of experiment, and the great weight seemed to trouble him as little as a fifty-pound pack would harass a white man. In the rivers he was not the equal of Jeddore, Matty Burke, or John Hinx, but the Indian nature is nothing if not acquisitive, for in a few days he worked his pole with considerable skill and untiring patience.[79]

John Hinx, intercepted the party on the river, arriving "tired and cheerful after a thirty-five mile walk from his 'tilt' ":

> John Hinx, a typical half-breed of an English father and Indian mother, is one of the most experienced men in the island. He has been all over the south and central portions, and has made his living by trapping and log-cutting since he was ten years of age, and is now fifty, though in appearance he might have passed for thirty-five. He became my cook and camp man, but was, nevertheless, an excellent hunter, and always accompanied Steve and me on our tramps after deer, when his sharp eyes were sometimes responsible for some outlying stag which we had overlooked. He possessed a great knowledge of the deer and their movements, and what he did not know of otters and otter-trapping was not of much account. He was tall and good-looking, spoke broken English, and, being fearful of being misunderstood, was at first somewhat reticent, but as time wore on he would chatter as freely as Steve, and entertain us with tales of flood and forest that always had some interesting point.[80]

The party poled and hauled their canoes upstream, past the "endless falls, boiling runs, and sudden 'drops' " past Hinx's tilt to Pudopsk, a chain of small lakes toward the headwaters.[81] Here Matty Burke and Johnny Benoit left them. They agreed to return in early November to help on the return journey. A few miles up from

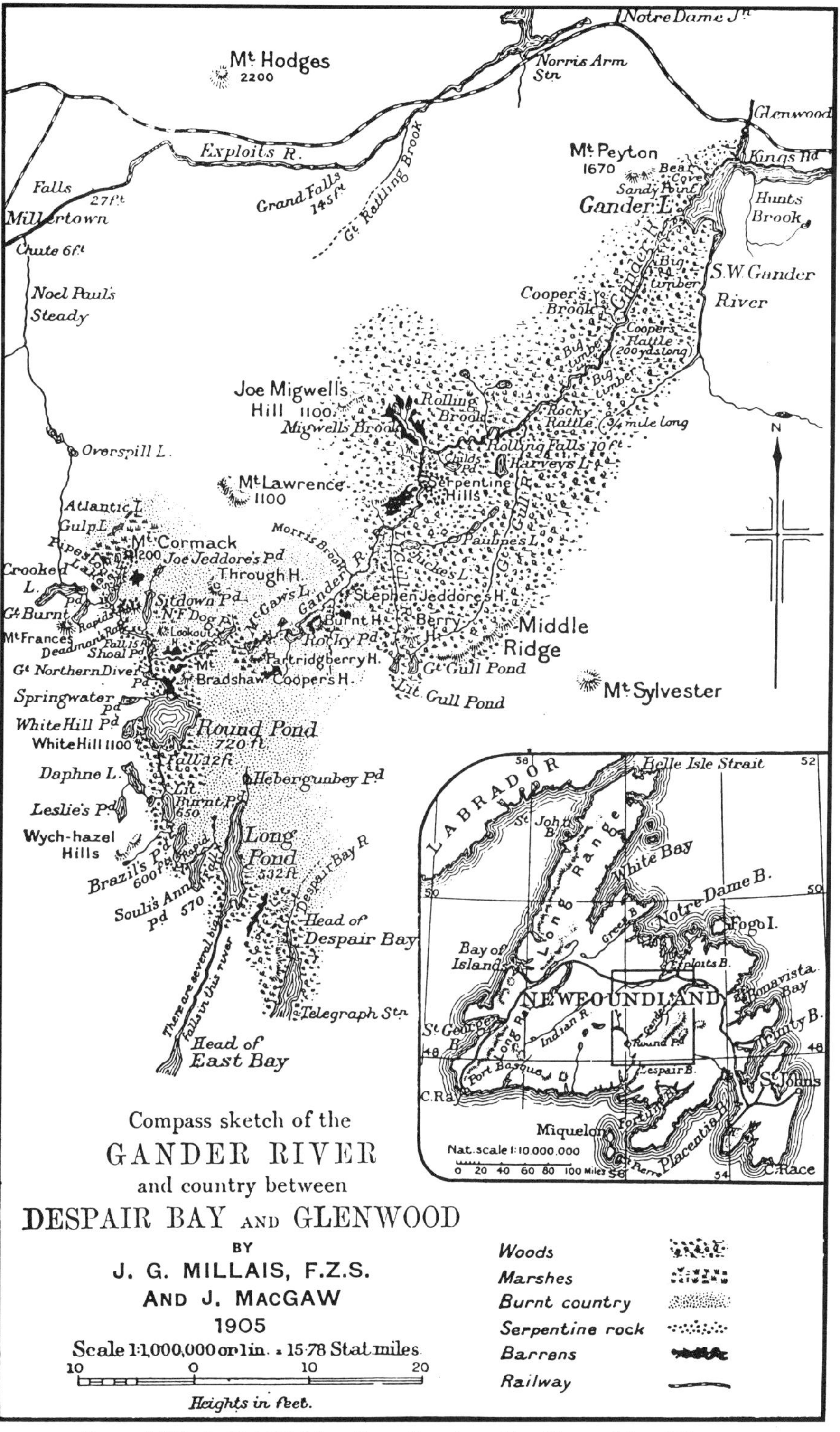

From Millais (1907) Newfoundland and its Untrodden Ways.

Pudopsk they stashed their canoes and struck west over the open country to Kesoquit Hills, the traditional hunting territory of the John family, Micky among them. Millais adopted as his base Kesoquit "droke," an island of woods where the Johns had a camp. A second camp near Shoe Hill Ridge was within Steve Bernard's family territory.

As Millais had suspected and as his guides well knew, this was ideal caribou country. Kesoquit, Shoe Hill, and to the north Mount Sylvester offered commanding views of the barrens. Here were the stags Millais sought. He had his pick of trophy racks, taking five of the largest including one huge 45-pointer:

> This closed my hunting for the year, and perhaps for ever in Newfoundland. . . . This season had surpassed all my previous expeditions, both in the way of success, and in the enjoyment of finding and stalking deer in an open country where no white man had ever hunted before. Others will doubtless come after me, and for them I can only wish the good luck that attended me; but I trust that they will employ the Indians who accompanied me, and whose lawful hunting-grounds lie within this area of the country.[82]

Serving with men like Howley, Kennedy and Millais, the Micmac acquired a considerable reputation as guides. A spate of publications urged sportsmen to employ the Micmac as "Indians are almost indispensable in these excursions."[83] A book on salmon fishing describes the "splendid fishing" on Conne Brook and notes that "Indians from the settlement make excellent guides for the river."[84] In *Sporting Notes*, Kennedy included advice on the appropriate provisions and gear for a caribou hunt, adding that "all these preparations are, in my opinion, useless without Indians to ensure success."

> The white men are very useful and necessary, but they know nothing about deer-stalking or the habits or whereabouts of the animal. The Indians are thoroughly familiar with the country, and are experienced hunters and trappers. . . . Some do not believe in Indians—say they are humbugs, and worse than useless. I have yet to learn what these individuals have done without them. I only speak from my own experience, and I would as soon attempt hunting in these countries without an Indian as without power.[85]

By way of an admonition he added:

> . . . but they are grasping and extortionate in their demands, and the best of them will not stir under $3 a day and his food. This seems preposterous, and I have got them for less; but then they said they would not go again for the money unless taken for a month, when they will go for $1.[86]

Perhaps the Micmac were as much pragmatic as ''grasping,'' for the trapline was equally profitable. Perhaps they were a little jealous or protective too, for it was their land, tribal land. As Millais noted, the Micmac is proud and independent, confident of his ability on the country and perhaps a little scornful of those less able. Sportsmen were assured a successful hunt only if they demonstrated respect and heeded the guide's instructions. Otherwise they could expect failure, or worse. One veteran guide, Peter Oliver of St. George's, said, ''Any English that went in the country with me kept his nose clean, or perhaps he wouldn't come out.'' Millais was told a story of one man who almost did not make it out, ''a loud blowin', bullyin' feller'' who had insulted his guide, Stephen, after some poor luck on the hunt:

> Stephe never sed a word at first, but jus' looks at 'un wi' his cold eyes, then he darts off, sayin' he'd show him deer for sure that day. They jus' walked and walked and walked, and by-and-by Stephe tells de feller to sit down and take a spell while he goes into the timber to light a fire and boil the kettle. Presently the man from Bonava's Bay gets cold and hungry, and he goes to find Stephe and de kittle; but de Indian was far away by that time, and he didn't ever see 'un again—least not for some time. . . .
>
> Well, if it hadn't bin that there was plenty blueberries that fall, and he had a box of matches, he certainly wouldn't a' seen Bonava's Bay agin, for he was clean lost. It took 'un three days 'fore he struck the Terra-Nova River, where some loggers picked 'un up famished and 'most crazy.[87]

NOTES

1. David McNab, ''The Micmac Nation and British Imperial Policy, 1713-1907'' (Unpublished paper, 1978), p. 3.
2. Edward Wix, *Six Months of a Newfoundland Missionary's Journal* (London: Smith, Elder and Co., 1836), p. 13.
3. Ibid., pp. 13-14.
4. Ibid., pp. 84-85.
5. Ibid., pp. 86-87.

6. Ibid., pp. 89-90.
7. Ibid., p. 101.
8. Jukes, *Excursions*, Vol. I, pp. 113-114.
9. Ibid., p. 121.
10. Ibid., p. 124.
11. Ibid., p. 125.
12. Ibid., p. 127.
13. Ibid., p. 129.
14. Ibid., pp. 132-133.
15. Ibid., pp. 138-139.
16. Ibid., pp. 144-146.
17. Ibid., pp. 149-150.
18. Ibid., p. 149.
19. Ibid., p. 149.
20. Ibid., p. 170.
21. Ibid., p. 176.
22. Ibid., pp. 173-175.
23. Ibid., vol. II, p. 1.
24. Ibid., pp. 105-106.
25. *Journal of the House of Assembly* (St. John's: Queen's Printer, 1852), p. 153.
26. Ibid., p. 153.
27. Ibid., p. 156.
28. Ibid., p. 166.
29. Ibid., p. 156.
30. Ibid., p. 156.
31. Ibid., p. 153.
32. Addison Bown, *Newfoundland Journeys* (New York: Carleton Press, 1971), p. 56.
33. *JHA*, 1864, p. 567.
34. Ibid., p. 529.
35. Ibid., p. 536.
36. Ibid., p. 537.
37. Ibid., p. 537.
38. Ibid., 1865, p. 722.
39. Ibid., 1864, p. 535.
40. Ibid., 1866, p. 690.

41. *Journal of the Legislative Council*, (St. John's: Queen's Printer, 1876), pp. 124-125.
42. Alexander Murray and James P. Howley, *Geological Survey of Newfoundland* (London: Edward Stanford, 1881). This volume includes their annual reports from 1864 to 1880.
43. Rogers, *Historical Geography*, p. 161.
44. Murray and Howley, *Geological Survey*, p. 188.
45. Ibid., p. 189.
46. Ibid., p. 205.
47. Ibid., p. 250.
48. Ibid., p. 354.
49. Ibid., p. 416.
50. Ibid., p. 416.
51. Ibid., pp. 426-427.
52. Ibid., p. 436.
53. *JHA*, 1876, p. 402. This brief survey, undertaken by a Mr. Bellairs, may or may not have involved Micmac guides. The author has been unable to track down any report related to the survey.
54. Father Michael Morris, "The Proposed Railway Across Newfoundland: A Lecture" (St. John's: *Public Ledger*, 1875), pp. 2, 5-6, 15.
55. *JHA*, 1876, p. 93.
56. Ibid., p. 94.
57. Ibid., p. 95.
58. *JLC*, 1877, p. 487.
59. Ibid., p. 529.
60. Howley, *The Beothucks*, p. 143.
61. Lieut. E. C. Kennedy, "After Caribou in Newfoundland," in *Newfoundland Quarterly*, 1904, December, Vol. IV, no. 3, p. 6. Cited from an introduction by D. W. Prowse.
62. Captain W. R. Kennedy, *Sport, Travel and Adventure in Newfoundland* (London: William Blackwood and Sons, 1885), p. 176.
63. Ibid., p. 177.
64. Ibid., pp. 178-179.
65. Captain W. R. Kennedy, *Sporting Notes in Newfoundland* (St. John's: Queen's Printer, 1881), pp. 14-15.
66. Millais, *Untrodden Ways*, p. 228.
67. Ibid., pp. 200-201.
68. Ibid., p. 202.
69. Ibid., p. 229.

70. Ibid., pp. 215-216.
71. Ibid., p. 216.
72. Ibid., p. 258.
73. Ibid., p. 262.
74. Ibid., p. 263.
75. Ibid., p. 267.
76. Ibid., p. 267.
77. Ibid., p. 268.
78. Ibid., p. 270.
79. Ibid., pp. 267-268.
80. Ibid., p. 271.
81. Ibid., p. 270.
82. Ibid., p. 305.
83. Rev. M. Harvey, *Newfoundland as it is in 1894: A Handbook and Tourists' Guide* (St. John's: Queen's Printer, 1894), p. 293.
84. C. H. Palmer, *The Salmon Rivers of Newfoundland* (Boston: Farrington Printing, 1928), p. 212.
85. Kennedy, *Sporting Notes*, p. 44.
86. Ibid., p. 44.
87. Millais, *Untrodden Ways*, p. 55.

CHAPTER 6

19th-century Micmac growth areas — Census returns — Bay St. George, White Bear Bay, Bay d'Espoir, Gander Bay and Hall's Bay — Colonization — Salmon depletion and caribou slaughter

The closing decades of the 19th century witnessed the culmination of an odyssey begun centuries before. Successive migrations of families and bands sought and found sanctuary in Newfoundland. These were predominantly Micmac, but included Montagnais, Abenaki, and probably even Beothuk. Collectively they achieved a remarkable synthesis, in a sense a recreation of those archaic peoples from whom they all descended. Through intermarriage and social intercourse they were bound by blood, language and lifestyle. They had secured an unchallenged occupation of their new homeland.

Pastore describes it as their "Indian summer . . . a reprieve from the fate which overtook all other Indians south of the St. Lawrence;"[1] the Malecite, Mohawk and Iroquois were all subjected to colonial settlement and industry. In Newfoundland they were able to carry on a traditional lifestyle, while Micmac in Cape Breton had abandoned their tribal lands which had become settlements, farms and factories. It was a temporary reprieve. Those conditions which had permitted their Indian summer were not precluded but merely postponed.

It is impossible to reconstruct Micmac population and distribution during this period. A baseline is Cormack's 1822 observation: a total of 27 or 28 families, 150 tribesmen, distributed among six settlements on the south, west and north coasts.[2] If these figures are accurate there must have been a counter-migration since the number arriving from Cape Breton after 1763 was larger than this.

Clearly the situation was in flux. There was a persistent pattern of migration and counter-migration across the Cabot Strait and the Strait of Belle Isle. Incoming families arrived in search of better hunting, perhaps reuniting with fellow kinsmen. Communication and comradeship between the Micmac of Newfoundland and Nova Scotia culminated in the formal institution of a Newfoundland chieftainship aligned with the Grand Council in 1860.

To some extent families alternated between fixed coastal sites and interior hunting camps. Summer coastal campsites were largely or wholly abandoned, presumably in response to European settlement. The association of particular families with a summer camp varied as a result of their nomadic habits.

Two sources help in this reconstruction although both have limitations for reasons that are interesting in themselves. The first is a history of contemporary Micmac families, tracing their origins via oral tradition supplemented by church records. Beyond the later years of the 19th century, memory fades and church records are incomplete. A confusing factor arises as Micmac family surnames are familiar as Christian names: Louis, Gabriel, John, Francis, Bernard, Joe and Paul. Speck notes that family and personal names "are often transposed; this causes some confusion to those who do not allow for this peculiarity."[3]* While it is assumed that contemporary families in Cape Breton and/or Newfoundland sharing the same family name are descended from a common ancestor, it is difficult to prove.

The second source is census returns. Regular census taking at ten-year intervals started in 1836. The enumeration forms have not survived. The reports are statistical tables indicating the total population of each settlement broken down by age, sex, occupation and the like. The names of those enumerated are lost.

The 1857 census enumerators were directed to take note of the Micmac population. The first notations appear in a "Miscellaneous" column of the abstracts where, for example, opposite the "Name of Settlement, Gander Bay," is found "3 male and 1 female Indians." In the case of Bay d'Espoir and Grandy's Brook the notation "(Indians)" is placed beside the name of the settlement and an explanatory note added in a miscellaneous column.

Through subsequent censuses these "Indians," sometimes specifically "Micmacs," were allotted their own column, "Male Indians/Female Indians." In 1884 they were returned to the miscellaneous column before disappearing from the census by 1911.

As helpful as this data may be, the figures are not an accurate indication of Micmac population and distribution.

* * * * *

---

*The classic example is Cormack's Joe (Joseph) Sylvester.

The major Micmac settlement of the late 18th and early 19th centuries was Bay St. George. Cormack stopped here in 1822 and mentions two houses which "belonged to Indians" including "the captain or chief's,"[4] Emanuel Gontgont. Nine years before, Lieutenant Edward Chappell of H.M.S. *Rosamond* noted 20 wigwams and a population of 97:

> The village appeared to be entirely deserted by the men; and the women and children, being naturally shy of strangers, fled into the woods at our approach.
>
> The wigwams, or habitations of the Micmac Indians, are constructed of birch-tree bark in a conical shape; and at the top there is an aperture for the smoke to escape through. They make their fires in the centre of the hut; and suspend deer-flesh over it, to dry for the winter consumption. . . . We also perceived great quantities of stinking fish and bones lying scattered about their wigwams; together with canoes, and large fish-stages.[5]

Chappell mentions a "grant of a sterile tract of land in St. George's Bay" awarded to Cape Breton Micmac during the American revolution. Unfortunately he does not give a source, nor is there evidence that English authorities honoured this commitment. Chappell states that the Micmac, "after boldly launching out to sea in their own crazy shallops or canoes . . . eventually reached St. George's Bay in safety" where their first act

> . . . was to appoint the old Indian, who had conducted them thither, their Chief in perpetuity; and they next "buried the sword," as a symbol that war had forever ceased between their tribe and the English nation.[6]

Reports from naval commanders and colonial authorities indicate that the population varied considerably; 30 families were recorded in 1788, 150 persons in 1794, 100 in 1797, 30 in 1801, 70 to 80 in 1810, and 66 in 1830.[7] These fluctuations are attributed to continuing traffic between Cape Breton and Bay St. George and dispersal to other sites.

One of Chappell's observations concerns intermarriage: "By frequent intermarriages with the European settlers at Sandy Point, the race became so intermingled, that, at the time we visited them, the number of pure Indians did not exceed fifty, exclusive of women and children."[8] Until 1904 the west coast was the French Shore and off limits to English settlement. Nevertheless there was a small number of English settler families, 32 in 1828, concentrated at Sandy Point directly opposite a Micmac campsite. By 1850 they were outnumbered by an influx of French settlers: Acadians, immigrants from St. Pierre and others directly from France.[9]

Elsewhere in Canada, a mix of French and Indian blood gave rise to the Métis. In Newfoundland people of that same mix are known as Jack-a-Tars, the English term originally used to denote a sailor.[10] The term is very much part of the idiom, used by Newfoundlanders to refer to these Indian-French people of Bay St. George.

They disappear from the written record during the late 19th century. This is not to say they actually vanished, but in the colonial record they are overlooked or ignored, presumably absorbed by European culture through marriage between French men (with surnames like le Blanc, le Jeune and Benoit) and Indian women.

There were three other sites on the French shore, the largest on the Great Codroy River. Cormack mentions ten Micmac families camped for the winter "about ten miles from its mouth."[11] Jukes met with the Indians but gave no indication of their numbers. Census enumerators recorded 24 males and 28 females in 1857; 8 males in 1869; 35 males and 12 females in 1874.[12] An influx of Cape Breton Scots to Codroy beginning about 1841[13] induced them to move.

Two minor sites, Bay of Islands and Bonne Bay, were "occasionally" frequented by Micmac in Cormack's time.[14] Little is known about either. One reference to the Bay of Islands is Jukes' account of the old tattooed woman, her two daughters and son-in-law. No references appear in the census of 1857. Indians appear in Bonne Bay in the census of 1891 when a single male is recorded.[15] This was Matty Mitchell, later acclaimed as an expert guide. His descendants recall that he hunted between Bonne Bay and the upper Humber River. Each year he took fur to Bay St. George for trade, and married a local Micmac girl. Speck records the "hereditary chieftaincy" of the Mitchells:

> On this account the Mitchells have the privilege of hunting almost anywhere without hindrance and even trapping inside of other claims if the proprietors themselves are not working at the time in the neighbourhood. . . . Within the last twenty years Mathew Mitchell has hunted in the Bonne bay district, which had hitherto been unoccupied by the Micmac.[16]

Early contacts between Micmac and Montagnais took place north of Bay St. George and inland. The lay of the land, particularly the course of the Humber River, drew Montagnais on the Great Northern Peninsula southwest to the coast. According to Speck, the families (including the Mitchells) who claimed hunting grounds in this area were of mixed Micmac and Montagnais ancestry.[17]

Census returns through the latter half of the century record few Indians on the Great Northern Peninsula; none are identified specifically as Montagnais. In 1857 one male and two female Indians were recorded between Quirpon and Cape Norman.[18] The 1884 census identified 26 Indians in six locations on the east and west shores of the Great Northern Peninsula.[19] By 1891 two remained, Matty Mitchell in Bonne Bay and a man on Sop's Island.[20]

Perhaps in a pattern similar to the early Micmac occupation, many were engaged in a seasonal migration across the Strait of Belle Isle, crossing over for a few months' hunting and trapping, then returning. Certainly some intermarried with local Micmac, perhaps settlers as well. One of Speck's informants reported:

> . . . twenty-five years ago (1889) a band of Montagnais, consisting of forty families, from the south coast of Labrador, crossing the straits of Belle Isle, settled on the northwest coast of the island above Bonne bay. They stayed there hunting beaver all winter.[21]

Two principal south-coast campsites are identified by Cormack, White Bear Bay and Bay d'Espoir. Strangely, White Bear Bay does not appear in any 19th century census. It had no settler population but was occupied by an Indian band during the early years of the century. There were the three families Cormack met in the interior. One other reference exists—an amusing quote from a Protestant clergyman. In 1827 Reverend Noall of the Wesleyan Missionary Society, posted to Grand Bank, toured settlements in Fortune and Hermitage bays:

> On my return to Gaultois, I found Captain Michell (as he calls himself), the Chief of the gang of Indians from White-Bear-Bay. On seeing me he instantly dropped on one knee, putting his right hand to his head. He was a very tall man, and looked the savage if provoked. He addressed me in the most vociferating language, and gave me to understand that he considered himself a Catholic.[22]

Noall also mentions ''the Indians belonging to Bay Despair (of whom there are eighteen families, and about a hundred persons).''[23]

Referring to a dream of converting those Micmac in neighbouring Bay d'Espoir (''they are only the dupes of those priests''), he suggests that this ''would at once open up a religious intercourse between much greater numbers at White-Bear-Bay.''[24]

According to the census this campsite was abandoned prior to 1857 (when ''Indians'' were first enumerated), the resident families dispersing, perhaps to Bay d'Espoir or west to Grandy's Brook.

Like White Bear Bay and Bay d'Espoir, Grandy's Brook (near Burgeo) offered easy access to the southern interior and caribou herds. In 1869 enumerators noted an Indian presence: 6 male and 5 female; 13 in 1874; 10 in 1884; and 14 in 1891.[25] The settler population was concentrated at Upper Burgeo; Grandy's Brook settlers never numbered more than ten. According to Rogers, the Micmac abandoned the site ''when Burgeo became populous, and concentrated themselves on Conne River.''[26]

Fortune and Placentia bays were occupied by Micmac during the early 18th century. Campsites established during the period of French control were abandoned as no historical source refers to Indians settled east of Hermitage Bay. The census returns identify only four men: 1869, one in Lamaline; 1884, two in Mortier Bay; 1874 and 1884, one at Black Duck River, near the mouth of Piper's Hole River.[27]

This last was John Barrington, a recent immigrant from Cape Breton. His descendants recall that his hunting territory was the Piper's Hole watershed. Millais confirms this in his list of Micmac hunters and their respective family grounds. It was this John Barrington who guided on the railway survey of 1875.

On the northeast coast, Micmac settlement is recent, never achieving the significance of south- and west-coast sites. Throughout the 18th century, the division of tribal territory with the Beothuk served as a buffer to Micmac expansion northeastward. Only at the close of the century did the Micmac securely extend their territory. The campsites in Clode Sound and Gander Bay mentioned by Cormack were founded by families from Bay d'Espoir.

The 1857 census recorded one female and three males in Gander Bay.[28] No Indians were recorded in Clode Sound or in Bonavista Bay that year. Howley includes a ''letter from the Micmac Indian, John Lewis,'' one of Cormack's guides, posted from Clode Sound in March of 1828 in which he refers to several families then camped there.[29] Indians appear in the 1884 census abstracts: seven men and four women (eight men and no women in 1891).[30]

Charles Francis, the guide employed by the geological survey and the postal service is identified in Gander Bay in 1864.[31] His descendants, who remain at Clarke's Head, recall that Francis and his mother were immigrants from Nova Scotia, first settling in Bay d'Espoir about mid-century. His family hunting ground was the main Gander River.

Wigwam Point is further along the northeast coast, in Notre Dame Bay, at the mouth of the Exploits River. Cormack does not mention it, but the site was established before his expedition. Lieutenant Buchan found at the mouth of Rattling Brook a canoe stash ''that belonged to the Canadians who had resided at Wigwam Point.''[32] Among those who accompanied Cull's expedition were ''two of the Micmac Indians'' who may well have been resident there.[33] In the 1857 census ''three Indian families comprising 23 in all'' were located in ''Exploits Bay.''[34] They disappear until 1884—nine males and six females—and 1891—eight males and no females.[35] Upstream from Wigwam Point, at the mouth of Badger Brook, another campsite is known from oral tradition only.

A surname associated with both sites is Paul, specifically John Paul of Badger and Noel Paul of Wigwam Point. Their relationship is unknown. The descendants of John Paul believe that he came from Grandy's Brook. Larry Paul, a descendant of Noel, is certain his family originated at Castor River on the Great Northern Peninsula. An unidentified report of a salmon warden has a ''Noel Paul'' fishing Grandy's Brook. The two families settled on the lower Exploits and its tributaries. Later in the century they were joined by one of John Barrington's sons who briefly shared territory with John Paul before claiming Badger Brook.

The largest campsite on the northeast coast was at Hall's Bay, where Kennedy acquired his guides. Census returns identified a total of 30 Indians in 1869 (14 male and 16 female), 26 in 1874 (sex unspecified), and 34 in 1884 (17 male and 17 female).[36] They disappeared from the 1891 census.

* * * * *

The early Newfoundland salmon fishery was prosecuted with nets stretched across a river mouth. While the substantial catch provided a profitable supplement, the harvest dropped as spawning runs were fished out. Sawmills posed an additional threat as dams blocked the salmon. In 1880, during one of his fishery patrols, Captain Kennedy discovered "in one bay alone" on the northeast coast "no less than thirty-six fine rivers completely barred by mill-dams, without so much as a trap or gate for the passage of fish . . . almost the whole of the noble salmon rivers are ruined."[37]

Protective legislation was belatedly passed. Law enforcement was confined to sporadic patrols by naval vessels whose captains, like Kennedy, were empowered as justices of the colony. Their efforts proved inadequate, as he noted, "it is impossible for them to be everywhere at once, and the nets are usually taken up on the appearance of a man-of-war, to be replaced as soon as she is out of sight."[38] Deputized wardens proved equally inadequate. They were often intimidated by culprits while those less conscientious were ravaging the salmon runs themselves.

Salmon was an important part of the Micmac diet, and the locations of coastal campsites were in part determined by access to a spawning run. Stream destruction disrupted this settlement pattern, particularly along the northeast coast. The abandonment of the Hall's Bay camp (site of at least one sawmill by the 1870s) might be attributed to this factor. Sites in Gander and Bonavista bays were ideally situated. Micmac families who might otherwise have stayed at those sites were deterred by salmoniers and loggers. The "serious complaints" made against Charles Francis might have been connected with salmon.

More important to the Micmac than the dwindling salmon stocks was the disruption of their livelihood on the country. There was a proliferation of forest fires during the latter decades of the century caused by northeast coast settlers on their seasonal forays in search of firewood. Murray charged that "such visits frequently, if not invariably terminate by setting fire to the woods."[39] In 1876 Howley described the course of "the most disastrous of the more recent fires":

> It originated near the main Gander River, about forty miles above the lake, and then swept nearly the entire space between the two rivers, until checked by the intervention of the Great Lake, which saved the lower valley. One stripe of this fire crossed the Southwest River a little above the forks, and pursuing an easterly course, ran through the country a few miles back of the southern shore of the lake, struck it at its eastern extreme, crossed to

> Freshwater Bay, and thence laid waste the entire northernside of Bonavista Bay. Another stripe of the same fire ran down the west side of the main branch of the Upper Gander, swept over Mount Peyton, which it laid bare, thence struck northerly, finally reaching the shores of the Bay of Exploits, where Messrs. Winsor and Vallance's saw-mill was caught in the flames and burnt to the ground.[40]

The fire, which burned over 2000 square miles, was attributed to "lumber explorers or 'rhynders' . . . omitting to extinguish their campfires, or smoke heaps, which they had used to drive off flies."[41]

Timberland in the Exploits Valley was similarly destroyed: "in a walk of something like sixty miles terminating up the Victoria River, I was seldom out of sight of burnt country."[42] These fires were started by logging crews clearing the road for the railway then under construction, as it was common practice to burn off brush and larger trees to ease their task.[43] Murray and Howley regretted the destruction of commercial timber, however the destruction of wildlife and habitat was enormous.

The railway precipitated the most disastrous impact on Micmac life: the caribou slaughter. The proposed route of 1875 was abandoned and a new route was chosen, arcing over the main body of the interior and terminating at Port aux Basques.

The new route intersected the caribou migration at its most concentrated point, the base of the Great Northern Peninsula. With White Bay to the east and Bonne Bay to the west, natural formations funnelled the southbound herds across a relatively short length of track. A natural phenomenon previously witnessed by a handful was now readily accessible to anyone with the price of a train ticket.

As word spread hundreds flocked each fall to meet the herds. From scores of campsites lining the tracks they ambushed the oncoming caribou. The butchered carcasses were loaded on passing trains for the homeward trip. This was the "annual bombardment at Howley," referring to the rail station where the slaughter was concentrated.[44]

The colony was unprepared for this. Public interest in wildlife was represented by two unofficial bodies, the Game Fish Protection Association and the Game Protection Society. When government passed legislation regulating the hunt (imposing non-resident licensing, a closed season and bag limits), the latter group was responsible for enforcement. The Society complained that it could do little to confront the "open violation of laws," laws condemned as "lax in construction and muddled in expression."[45] The funds provided it, a small portion of the licence fees, were inadequate. Members requested an increased budget, asking for the entire licence fund "as a premium of insurance for the protection of a precious asset." Government continued to use licence sales as a source of general revenue.[46] When enforcement was transferred to the Marine and Fisheries department, administration of the licence fund and appointment of wardens became enmeshed in petty politics and patronage. Critics charged that district wardens were being removed on account of their "political apathy or suspected hostility to the party in power."[47] Scandal prompted action. The Game and Inland Fisheries Board was established in 1906. Even so appointments were not made until 1909.[48]

Still the slaughter continued, the Board powerless to intervene. Its 1914 annual report gives this assessment:

> The large area to be covered, the irregular movements and migrations of the herds, and the distribution of the Deer over such a large area, and the fact of many places being almost inaccessible, make it impossible for the Board, with the limited number of men at its disposal, to arrive at conclusions of any statistical value (i.e., accurately determining the numbers killed). Generally speaking, however, it is very apparent that the Caribou Herds are being very rapidly reduced in numbers, and that the total number of Deer slaughtered is very much beyond any figures gathered and reported by the officials employed by the Board.[49]

The slaughter was not confined to the bottleneck area or to Newfoundlanders alone. The trickle of intrepid sportsmen like Millais, the Earl of Dunraven and F. C. Selous escalated into a substantial tourism industry. Millais published *Newfoundland and Its Untrodden Ways* in 1907, and Radclyffe Dugmore produced *The Romance of the Newfoundland Caribou*[50] in 1913. The island acquired a reputation for trophy caribou. Entrepreneurs established as outfitters, organizing "little armies of sportsmen at $200 a head." Hesketh Prichard complained, "The 'opening up' of Newfoundland came suddenly and swiftly. . . ."[51] Rail stations at Gambo, Terra Nova, Glenwood, Badger and Howley were staging points. At Terra Nova Lake, where Prichard had hunted earlier in privacy, he encountered five parties of sportsmen in 1906.[52]

Hunting near Sandy Lake, American E. J. House encountered similar concentrations; the silence of the woods was broken by "the continual crackling of firearms as these parties took their toll from the migrating herds."[53] Kennedy bemoaned the fact that fellow Englishmen, "calling themselves sportsmen, have also been guilty of this butchery, one party having, some years ago, massacred over a hundred, leaving their carcases to rot under the ground."[54] Millais reported that "conducted parties, numbering fifty men in each party, are now coming from America each year, and who knows what number this may reach."[55]

This was slaughter on a grand scale with a majority of sportsmen interested in the trophy rack only. For a time there was a brisk traffic in caribou heads; local merchants and taxidermists outfitted hunters to scour the country for stags.[56] "Market hunters" and their considerable trade in caribou meat were reported by the Game Board in 1914:

> Recent evidence, that appears quite reliable, goes to show that in some localities (which the Board has been unable to warden owing to lack of funds), where Deer are found practically throughout the year, they are being slaughtered at all seasons and are used, not alone as an article of food by the killers but also as an article of Traffic, and sold in adjacent localities with which there is steam communication.[57]

The arrangement was "a kind of grub-stake affair":

> The hunters are fitted out by a local man with powder, shot and provisions, he paying himself out of the proceeds of the trip. The method is this: the hunters go up as far as possible into the country by boat, and camp. They then scatter all over the hills till a herd is found, when the whole party starts together, and one man takes charge. His business is to place the men, with guns, in the different leads, one man in each; and when all is ready he goes round to the windward of the herd and starts driving them towards the leads. The waiting hunter shoots the leading deer, the others turn back to another lead to be met in the same manner, and so on till the deer become so frightened that they flock together, and are often nearly all killed by the hunters who have closed in round them. The number taken would not nearly represent the number destroyed, as about sixty per cent are does which would in a few weeks drop their fawns, and many wounded would escape to die in agony in the bush. When the hunters are satisfied—that is when they can get no more—the

> carcasses are taken to the edge of the ice to be left there till the steamer calls for them. If mild weather prevails, many are thrown away; but, if frosty, the meat comes to St. John's fresh.[58]

Fresh meat was sold for pennies a pound; meat that spoiled in transit, as frequently happened, was dumped.[59]

The caribou slaughter and the invasion of the interior were accelerated by industrial development. The most important was the creation of the Anglo-Newfoundland Development Company (A.N.D.), a large British-owned newsprint operation. Incorporated in 1905, A.N.D. was granted a site on the Exploits River (now Grand Falls) and constructed the mill. It was allotted timber concessions of 2000 square miles. By 1925 the company had acquired a second site (Bishop's Falls), spawned the logging towns of Terra Nova, Badger and Millertown, and expanded its timber holdings to over 7000 square miles.[60] Caribou were exploited by logging crews for fresh meat for the camps on the Expoits, Gander and Terra Nova rivers. Despite evidence of a substantial reduction the government issued permits to A.N.D. authorizing killing as required.[61]

As the plight of the caribou became apparent, some blamed the Micmac for the slaughter. The tribe had become more visible, particularly those settled on the Exploits and Gander rivers. Aside from guiding, they lived as hunters and trappers, apt to disappear for months and reappear with bundles of fur and caribou.

It was sportsmen who came to their defence. Prichard states that while the Micmac were "popularly supposed by the settlers to 'kill all they can come up with,' it is quite probable that they are far more economical of animal life than their white brethren."[62] Kennedy was emphatic:

> The Indians are often accused of slaughtering deer in a whole sale way; but of this I feel confident they are guiltless. The deer and beaver supply them with food, and they could not exist without them; therefore it is their interest to protect them, killing merely what they require. Not so the white settlers, who openly boast of the number they slaughter in the winter time for the sake of their hides and horns.[63]

Millais insisted that "Indians are not wasteful in their methods, far less so than the white man, as every part of a deer is used, and they never kill one unless it is for some special purpose."[64]

Caribou herds were reduced but were not entirely destroyed. While it seemed to some that they verged on extinction, judging from the number crossing the railway each fall, there remained the southern herd, whose limited migration north fell short of the railway. The cumulative effect of the railway slaughter was a progressive fragmentation of herds now isolated in pockets between Bonavista, Notre Dame and White bays and on the Great Northern Peninsula. Local hunters reduced their numbers as the southern herd was hemmed in by the advance of logging crews.

These developments served to fragment and isolate the Micmac. Campsites at Glenwood and Badger became rail and logging towns; native families were submerged under an influx of settlers. On the west coast, in Bay St. George, the settlers previously concentrated on Sandy Point moved to sites along the tracks. The northern interior was shattered by the "crackling of guns" and the ring of the logger's axe. Larry Paul of Wigwam Point, back from the first world war, returned to Exploits River to find it invaded by an "army of sports; [their firing] just a steady roar, . . . like I was back on the western front." There were few caribou along the Exploits, fewer still to the north and west. Traditional Indian land use ceased, for without caribou the hunter could not support family or maintain traplines. Families at Gander Bay, Glenwood, Badger, Wigwam Point and Bay St. George, removed from traditional subsistence patterns, were bound to a cash economy.

Country skills still served the Micmac well. There was a demand for experienced woodsmen on surveys, as loggers and guides. Some were renowned. Matty Mitchell is known as the discoverer of the mineral deposit at Buchans. The Johns of Glenwood, particularly James and Louis, were known as expert guides.

Conne River alone remained untouched by industrial development. Its hunting grounds lay beyond the reach of developers. Just as the Newfoundland Micmac escaped temporarily the colonial development taking place on the mainland, those at Conne River earned a second reprieve, emerging as the major Indian settlement on the island.

NOTES

1. Pastore, *Newfoundland Micmacs*, p. 24.
2. Howley, *The Beothucks*, p. 151.
3. Speck, *Beothuk and Micmac*, p. 134.
4. Howley, *The Beothucks*, pp. 158, 159.
5. Chappell, *Voyage*, pp. 74-75.

6. Ibid., p. 78.
7. John J. Mannion, "Settlers and Traders in Western Newfoundland," in John J. Mannion, ed., *The Peopling of Newfoundland* (St. John's: Memorial University of Newfoundland, 1977), p. 237.
8. Chappell, *Voyage*, p. 78.
9. Mannion, "Settlers," p. 234.
10. Peter Kemp, ed., *The Oxford Companion to Ships and the Sea* (London: Oxford University Press, 1976), p. 422.
11. Ibid., p. 163.
12. Provincial Archives of Newfoundland and Labrador (PANL), Census, 1857, p. 123; Census, 1869, Electoral District, French Shore; Census, 1874, p. 151.
13. Rosemary E. Ommer, "Highland Scots Migration to Southwestern Newfoundland: A Study of Kinship," in Mannion, *The Peopling*, p. 215.
14. Howley, *The Beothucks*, p. 151.
15. PANL, Census, 1891, p. 247.
16. Speck, *Beothuk and Micmac*, p. 135.
17. Ibid., pp. 132-134.
18. PANL, Census, 1857, p. 119.
19. PANL, Census, 1884, p. 205.
20. PANL, Census, 1891, p. 211.
21. Speck, *Beothuck and Micmac*, p. 126.
22. Rev. Philip Tocque, *Newfoundland as it Was, and as it is in 1877* (Toronto: John B. Magurn, 1878), p. 200.
23. Ibid., p. 200.
24. Ibid., p. 201.
25. PANL, Census, 1874, p. 139; 1884, p. 205; 1891, p. 301.
26. Rogers, *Historical Geography*, p. 164.
27. PANL, Census, 1869, Electoral District, Burin, 1874, p. 103; 1884, p. 145.
28. PANL, Census, 1857, p. 55.
29. Howley, *The Beothucks*, p. 203.
30. PANL, Census, 1884, p. 205; 1891, p. 277.
31. PANL, Census, 1869, Electoral District, Fogo.
32. Howley, *The Beothucks*, p. 73.
33. Ibid., p. 69.
34. PANL, Census, 1857, p. 63.
35. PANL, Census, 1884, p. 89; 1891, p. 187.

36. PANL, Census, 1869, Electoral District, Fogo; 1874, p. 83; 1884, p. 93.
37. Kennedy, *Sporting Notes*, pp. 25-26.
38. Ibid., p. 27.
39. Murray and Howley, *Geological Survey*, p. 361.
40. Ibid., p. 449.
41. Ibid., p. 449.
42. G. D. McGrigor, *Impressions of Newfoundland During a Journey in 1898*, (The Nelwyn Press, 1900?), p. 4.
43. Stanley Gillingham, personal communication, 1979.
44. Millais, *Untrodden Ways*, p. 3.
45. A. J. W. McNeily, ''Game and Game Fish Protection in Newfoundland,'' *Newfoundland Quarterly*, 1910, July, Vol. X, no. 1, p. 5.
46. Ibid., p. 5.
47. Ibid., p. 6.
48. Ibid., p. 6.
49. *Report of the Game and Inland Fisheries Board, Newfoundland, 1914*, (St. John's: Gray and Goodland, 1915), p. 8.
50. Dugmore, *Newfoundland Caribou.*
51. H. Hesketh Prichard, *Hunting Camps in Wood and Wilderness* (London: Thomas Nelson and Sons, 1910), p. 204.
52. Ibid., pp. 204-205.
53. Edward J. House, *A Hunter's Camp-fires* (New York: Harper and Brothers, 1909), p. 97.
54. Kennedy, *Sporting Notes*, p. 16.
55. Millais, *Untrodden Ways*, p. 333.
56. Prichard, *Hunting Camps*, p. 204.
57. *Report, Game and Inland Fisheries*, p. 8.
58. W. A. B. Sclater, ''The Woodland Caribou,'' *Newfoundland Quarterly*, 1905, July, Vol. V, no. 1, p. 10.
59. McGrigor, *Impressions*, p. 17.
60. *A.N.D. Facts and Figures*, No. 3, January, 1960 (Grand Falls).
61. Stanley Gillingham, personal communication, 1979.
62. Prichard, *Hunting Camps*, pp. 207-208.
63. Kennedy, *Sporting Notes*, p. 15.
64. Millais, *Untrodden Ways*, p. 221.

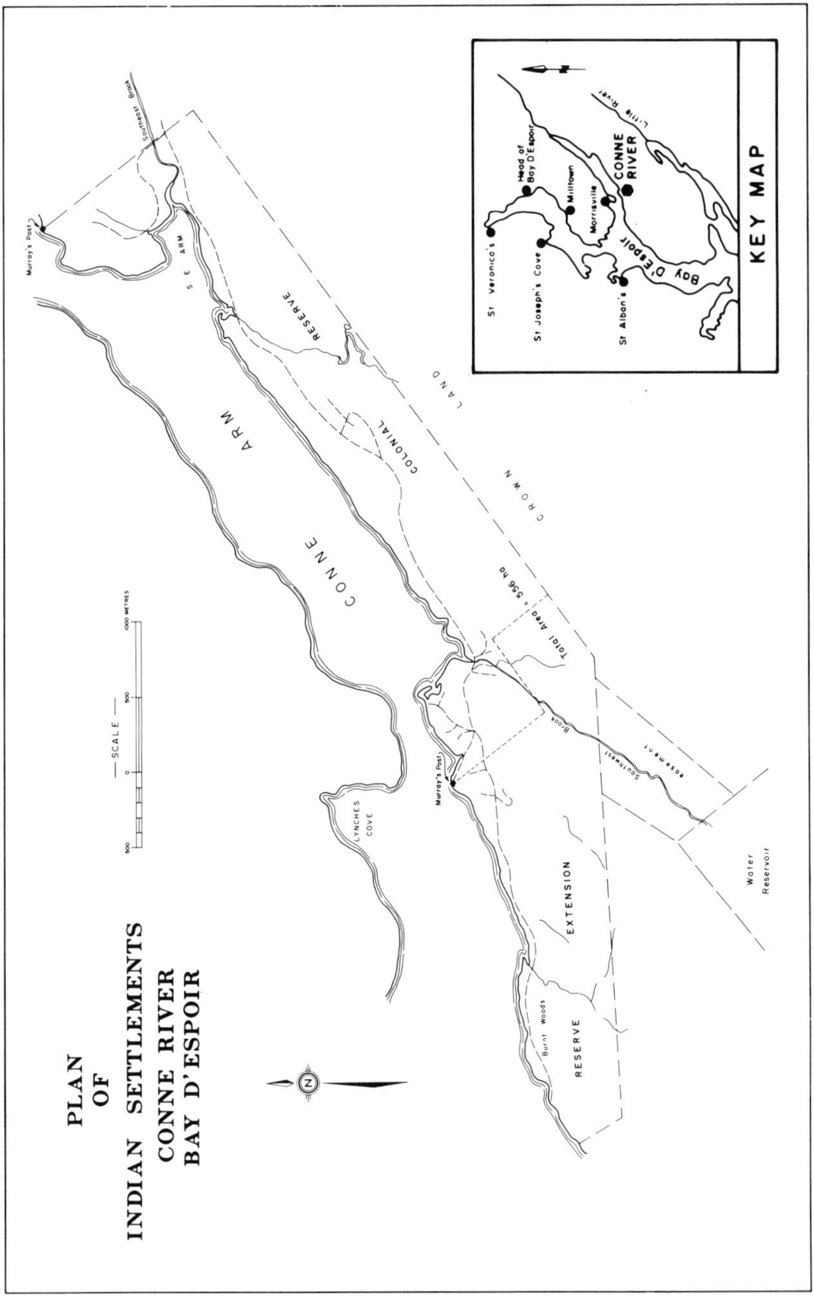

Samiajij Miawpukek Indian Reserve, 1987.

CHAPTER 7

Emergence of Conne River — Bishop Fleming's visit — Census of Bay d'Espoir — Governor MacGregor's visit — Colonial reserve — Micmac land

The south coast of Newfoundland presents a barren rugged face to the Atlantic, an imposing escarpment broken by jagged fiords and poor harbours. Midway across the island the shoreline arcs 30 miles inland, outlining Bay d'Espoir, an anglicization of Baie d'Espoir, or Bay of Hope. Short of the northern extremity, Conne Arm branches eastward through a ''gut'' or narrows, then widens briefly at the mouth of Conne Brook. The shore of this arm adjacent to the gut is the village of Conne River. Six settler communities occupy the opposite shore of Bay d'Espoir.

The first historical association of Micmac with Bay d'Espoir is Palliser's anxious announcement of 1766, informing the British Admiralty that a party of some 200 had landed there. For hunters there were advantages here. The bay neatly bisects caribou feeding grounds, two expanses of barrens between the Grey and Salmon rivers to the west and above Fortune and Placentia bays to the east. Proximity to big game, especially in winter, was essential. The Salmon and Bay du Nord rivers converge on Bay d'Espoir with Conne Arm positioned midway. Both offered access to prime hunting and trapping grounds. Conne Brook and Southeast Brook supported salmon, trout, geese and ducks. The gut abounded with eels, a favourite Micmac food. The forested slopes of the bay provided shelter, firewood and small game.

European interest in Bay d'Espoir focused on a single resource: timber. Elsewhere along the south coast forests were sparse and stunted. Bay d'Espoir had large stands of softwood and hardwood. The French logged here for ships' masts, planking and other materials for use at Placentia and St. Pierre. After the Treaty of Utrecht, the English expanded the harvest as the demand for wood grew.[1]

For both English and French, forestry was a seasonal pursuit. Crews hired by major trading companies overwintered, returning in the spring to Hermitage and Fortune bays. Others, including schooner crews, logged over the summer months. Permanent settlement was precluded by the area's isolation from fishing grounds.

In the latter half of the 19th century it supported a settler population involved in lumbering and subsistence agriculture, not fishing.

The Micmac occupied the bay in a number of temporary family campsites throughout its upper reaches. They regularly shifted camps, alternating between the coast in summer and the interior in winter.

Families from Bay St. George relocated to Bay d'Espoir in the early 19th century. Among them was Maurice Louis, whom Wix hired as a guide in 1835 (and possibly the man identified by Jukes as the discoverer of the Codroy coal). An unknown travelling missionary met Louis at Conne Arm and suggested that Louis encourage his people to gather there so that the church might serve them. This Louis did, laying the foundation of today's community.

In the first half of the 19th century references to the Micmac of Bay d'Espoir were made by two other churchmen. Rev. Simeon Noall of the Wesleyan Missionary Society toured Protestant communities in Hermitage and Fortune bays in 1827. At Gaultois Noall reported:

> I am informed by those who know their habits well, that the Indians belonging to Bay Despair (of whom there are eighteen families, about a hundred persons) are still under the bondage of the vilest habits; very indolent and false in their dealings; and there is too much reason to fear that they murder a great many of the Aborigines, or Red Indians, who inhabit the interior. After all, I think them an interesting race of men, and who, if they could be properly instructed, might emerge from that darkness in which they are now enveloped. At present they are only the dupes of those priests by whom they have been baptized, but never instructed. Although they are bound together by some social order, and have a sort of cantonment, or rather rendezvous, in Bay Despair, yet they enjoy very few of the comforts of civilized life.[2]

Bishop Michael Fleming visited in the summer of 1835. Most of his account is included:

> We passed along the coast of the charming Isle du Bois; and sailing by the mouth of Little River, at length came in sight of the Indian wigwams at the entrance of Conne River early in the day.
>
> These present a singular appearance to the stranger. Imagine to yourself a large collection of tents irregularly disposed,

constructed of long straight poles stuck in the ground and coming together at the top, tied with birch fastenings, and the whole kept in a circular form by means of hoops within and covered with the bark of trees.

At the entrance of the river a high sand-bank runs across, leaving barely room for a vessel to enter the pond or basin within [the gut], and upon this peninsular bank are those conical tents or wigwams disposed.

Upon our approach the inhabitants fled, but the instant we hoisted the flag, on which a cross was displayed, to the masthead, confidence seemed restored, and they returned from the woods.

And what was my annoyance to learn that, although these poor people had been two months expecting me in this place, for they had heard of my intended route to the westward even before they received my message, some evil-disposed person acquainted them, as if from authority, that no clergyman would visit them this year.

A few men and women, however, could not be dissuaded from waiting, so that in place of meeting at this rendezvous from two to three hundred Indians, I only found twenty-eight persons, whose joy in seeing us was testified by a thousand little innocent extravagances.

We remained with them till the following Wednesday, instructed them through an interpreter, said Mass every day in their wigwams, heard their confessions, and finally confirmed twenty-seven of their number, the others having been confirmed fifty years ago in Canada.

The simplicity of the manners of these people is truly interesting; and their piety, the air of recollection they exhibit at their devotions, their attachment to their religion, and their veneration for its ministers, are edifying in the extreme. In rearing their children they are particularly careful to instil into their tender minds a love of purity and attachment to every virtue.

Wherever they settle for a season, for they lead a wandering life, the first thing they do is to unite, and by their joint labour erect a large wigwam, which they use as a house of prayer; and should any of their tribe offend against public morals, he is invariably excluded from this church, and, in some cases, is never again permitted to enter until his offence is wiped away in the Sacrament of Penance; and they invariably observe the Sabbath with the most scrupulous exactness.

> On Sundays and holy days of the year they invariably assemble together in the morning, and after singing Kyrie Eleison, the Gloria, and Credo, they offer the Rosary, and some other prayers, usually occupying an hour; and in the afternoon they again meet and sing Vespers, for they have not only books of devotion written in their own language, but also the principal hymns and psalms set to the Gregorian chant.

Fleming wrote of his leavetaking:

> And now came the period of departure, and nothing could exceed the grief of the entire number, which vented itself alternately, amid sighs and tears, in treaties to prolong our stay, and complaints of the shortness of our visit.
>
> But on the morning of Wednesday, when our colours were hoisted, and they saw us determined to sail, they all turned out with long strand guns, and saluted us with several volleys, fired with the most unerring exactness, and several *feus de joie*, that seemed to betray long practice. The dexterity of the women in loading and firing the heavy pieces, seven or eight feet long, was particularly amusing to us and as long as we continued in sight, the warlike compliments were continued quicker in succession than it is possible to conceive.[3]

The dramatic reception suggests that visits by Catholic missionaries were rare. French clergy served the Micmac, who journeyed to St. Pierre.

A parish was created at Harbour Breton, the fishing centre of Fortune Bay, in 1856. Priests occasionally toured Bay d'Espoir and landed at Conne River. One priest, Father Nolan, a "great man for the country," often requested to be taken caribou hunting while in the village. Such visits were infrequent since many children born in the later years of the century were not baptized until age eight or more. Voyages to the French islands had ceased by this time.

At one time village elders kept a book in which they recorded important information, but it has not survived. A few items survive based on a 1936 translation by Joe Jeddore:

> The first Holy Mass was celebrated at Conne in a very rough dwelling house by celebrant —[name unknown]— in the year 1841. . . .
>
> The first ground was consecrated at Conne in the year 1864. A burying ground in use at that time was a place called Weasel Island in another branch of the bay. . . .

> The first chapel was built at Conne in the year 1871. This was the first Chapel built in Bay d'Espoir. . . .[4]

Visiting priests were sometimes guided inland to "mission rock" (location unknown) where they met northeast-coast Micmac for church services.

It is difficult to establish the size of the band during this period. Given their nomadic lifestyle and dispersed campsites, Noall's estimated 100 or Fleming's 200 to 300 are not reliable figures. The first formal census in 1836 makes no mention of Conne River or any community in the bay. The 1845 census records nine families in "Bay Despair," identifying one as Catholic, the remainder being Protestant Episcopalian.[5] Either enumerators did not land at Indian camps or the Micmac were camped elsewhere. In reports submitted by naval captains patrolling the south coast there are incidental references to an "Indian settlement," to "Indians, untidy, wigwams dirty"[6] and the like, but little substantive information. One report commented that "as they are always changing their abode," their number varied from three to twenty families.[7] In the four censuses following 1847, both "Conne River" and "Indians" are listed. Unless the enumeration was done at the height of the summer salmon run, families camped elsewhere missed being counted.

The Protestant Episcopalians appear in the 1840s, the start of a steady migration of European families to Bay d'Espoir. Many were veterans of the merchant logging crews, already familiar with the area. Some fished and farmed, virtually all logged, bartering timber for food and necessities with merchants and trading schooners. The table below shows the immigrant population had surpassed that of the Micmac by 1875.

Encroachment accelerated the concentration of Indian families along Conne Arm. Some were displaced from hunting and trapping grounds to the north and west of the arm as settlers took up the hunt and trapline. Some settlers were taught the country by Micmac who took them on as apprentices and temporary partners.

Census [8]

	1857	**1861**	**1874**	**1884**
Indian Population	55	88	79	77

Size of Settlement by Families[9]

	1855	1860	1865	1870	1875	1880	1885	1890
Conne River	?	9	?	22	12	?	18	14
Ship Cove (Now St. Alban's)	2	3	4	5	8	15	23	29
Head Bay d'Espoir			?	3	3	3	4	8
Head of Conne		1	1	1	1	1	2	2
Burnt Woods				1	1	1	1	1
St. Veronica				1	1	1	1	2
St. Joseph's					1	1	1	1

Indian families gradually abandoned their traditional wigwams in favour of wooden frame houses. Intermarriages between Indian men and white women tended to make the lifestyle of the community less migratory. They chose to remain in the village year round, while their husbands and sons pursued the hunt.

It was in the midst of this period that Alexander Murray began his expeditions up the Salmon River and made a legal survey of the Micmac village. The nature and circumstances of this survey remain a mystery, and two contradictory accounts exist, one a traditional account of the Micmac, the other a 1908 government report by Sir William MacGregor, who wrote:

> The Reservation, it appears, was laid off for the Micmacs about 1872, by Mr. Murray, Geological Surveyor of the Colony. It contained 24 blocks of about 30 acres each, with a water frontage of 10 chains. From the copy of the Reservation enclosed herewith it will be noticed that each parcel was to form the subject of a personal grant to the individual whose name is on the allotment. The right then conferred was in each case a "license to occupy" of which I enclose a copy in blank form. The license, it will be observed, would, on the fulfilment of certain conditions, have been replaced by a grant in fee, after five years. . . ."[10]

According to the terms, individuals would be granted title on condition that they occupy the land and cultivate a certain number of acres within a given period.

A contradiction arises in the Governor's report. The 1921 census includes individuals whose names on the survey plan indicate they were infants at the time of Murray's visit. Clearly MacGregor mistakenly identified Murray as the man who issued the licences. Indeed it is not certain that he actually surveyed the parcels, or the reserve boundary at all. The licenses were issued and the names affixed to the plan after Murray's original survey.

The reserve plan bears little resemblance to actual settlement. The majority of families were concentrated in the neighbourhood of Southwest Brook at the bottom or southwest end of the surveyed block. William Drew, Steve Bernard and John Denny Jeddore were issued licences to land which they did not occupy, and never would. Most of the land enclosed within the boundary to the northeast is steep, heavily forested, and unsuitable for agriculture. Yet, the terms of the licence obliged every family to cultivate land. MacGregor noted, "These Micmac are hunters and trappers, and are ignorant alike of agriculture, of seamanship, and of fishing."[11] He also found that "In few cases, if in any, have the terms of the license been complied with, and no grant in fee or other title has been issued to any of the occupants on this Reservation."[12] No one in Conne River possesses, or has ever possessed, title to any land within the boundary.

Village elders maintain that the land was granted to the Chief to hold in trust as common land. The Micmac had little understanding of or experience with land as private property. As trustee in the name of the people the Chief alone had authority to judge rights of occupation.

This tradition was consistently enforced. European families settled with the consent of the Chief. A note on the survey map shows that James MacDonald occupied parcel #23 "by permission of" the Chief. When this family erected a fence across a community path to Conne Brook, they were ordered to operate a gate. The Chief's permission was required when outsiders wished to haul logs, notably birch for barrel staves. When intruders attempted to slip in, elders recall, they were confronted and "driven off." The block was acknowledged by neighbouring white communities as

"Micmac land." The governor referred to Conne River as a "Reservation."

Why did Murray conduct the survey? If he acted under government direction there is no documentation. Did the Chief request the survey in the hope of stemming encroachment? Did Murray act independently? Was the survey an unconditional grant bestowed by the Crown? As a pioneering surveyor acquainted with Micmac people, he may have initiated the survey to secure a base from which they could continue to hunt and trap. No one pursued Murray's initiative, and no further action was taken to entrench Micmac rights.

Murray's survey was a recognition of the Newfoundland Micmac, as was MacGregor's 1908 visit. A humanitarian, MacGregor actively promoted Micmac interests. In 1905 he toured Inuit villages on the Labrador coast and was shocked by the ill treatment afforded them by government apathy. He visited Conne River to assess the situation of the Micmac. Excerpts from his report describe the circumstances and concerns of the community:

> The Micmac settlement is on a reservation situated on the Eastern side of the Conne arm of the Bay, with a frontage to the water of 230 chains, with an average depth of about 30 chains. It is on the slope of a wooded hill which is generally steep down to the sea, and at most places hard and rocky, covered by spruce forest. Most of the Micmac houses are on an area of about a quarter of a mile, where the ground is least steep and most suitable for building and gardening.
>
> In Appendix 1 hereto is given a list of the 23 families, consisting of 130 persons now living on the reservation; and of the 7 persons that have left it for Glenwood in this Colony. Two years ago three families left the Reservation to settle at Lewisport, and have not returned.
>
> These Micmacs are hunters and trappers, and are ignorant alike of agriculture, of seamanship, and of fishing. There is not more than three or four acres of cultivated land in the whole settlement. The greatest cultivator would not grow in one year more than three or four barrels of potatoes and a few heads of cabbage. There are two miserable cows in the place, and some of the least poor Micmacs possess three or four extremely wretched sheep. They have practically no fowls, but I saw one fowl and a tame wild goose. Their houses are small and inferior, of sawn timber, but have windows of glass. A few hundred yards of road,

constructed at the expense of the Government, traverses the end of the settlement where most of the people reside.

The community is Roman Catholic, and they have a small church, decently well built and kept, on the best site on the Reservation. It is built of sawn timber and would contain nearly one hundred people, which is too small for the festival of St. Anne, the patroness of the congregation. Over the entrance to the church there is printed in large characters, in the Micmac language, a total prohibition against spitting in Church.

The cemetery immediately adjoins the church, and there they bury their dead as members of a single family.

They have had a small school open since the 17th January last. It is a wooden room, about 12 by 15 feet, by no means new, with a small stove and two little windows.

The teacher is a woman of partly Micmac origin. She receives some very small allowance from the Parish Priest, and a few of the children, she says, pay some small fees. There are 34 children on the roll, and the winter attendance was from 25 to 30. They are divided into three classes, the highest of which could read slowly, in English, words of three or four letters. About half of them could write a little, a few of them surprisingly well on such brief tuition. The teacher says they are very amenable to discipline. Seldom has a school been started under greater difficulties than this Micmac institution. I was able to sincerely congratulate the teacher on what she has been able to accomplish under such unfavourable circumstances. It is manifest that the children are bright and clever, and that they would become useful and intelligent citizens if they had ordinary educational advantages. In this probably lies the best hope of a future prospect for this community. The settlement is visited now once a month by the Parish Priest; and in his absence, one of themselves, Stephen Jeddore, reads the service on Sunday. Last year they were visited by the Right Reverend Bishop McNeil.

They appear to be a comparatively healthy people. So far as known, no one is at present affected by tuberculosis in any form. I saw one woman of ninety years of age, Sarah Aseleka, perhaps the only Micmac of pure blood in the settlement. She was born at Bay St. George, and came to Bay d'Espoir some three score of years ago when the Micmacs first settled in this bay. The next oldest person is John Bernard, who is about eighty. Few of them were even fairly well clothed; the majority were in rags. A few wore homemade deer-skin boots, but most of them had purchased ready-made boots or shoes. They make deerskin boots by scraping caribou skin, and tanning it in a decoction of spruce bark. Such boots are, they state, worn through in a few days. The women can spin wool, and knit stockings. Their food consists chiefly of flour, a few potatoes, some cabbage, and perhaps about half a score of caribou a year for each family, hung up on trees and thus frozen during the winter. They also smoke fish, principally freshwater fish, and obtain a few grouse and hares, but, this small game has almost disappeared from the district. They have to go inland a score of miles to obtain caribou for food.

The principal Chief is Olibia, but I unfortunately did not meet him. He had gone out in March to his trapping ground near Mount Sylvester, but could not then reach his traps on account of the unusually great quantity of snow, and he had returned thither at the time of my visit.

I was informed that he was selected as Chief by the Micmacs of the Reservation, and was appointed by the principal Micmac Chief at St. Anne's, Nova Scotia, and by the Priest. I was shewn the insignia of office worn on ceremonial occasions by the Chief. It consists of a gold medallion with a chain attached, the whole in a case covered by red velvet. The medallion is inscribed "Presented to the Chief of the Micmacs Indians of Newfoundland," but with neither name nor date. The community paid for this badge of office forty-eight dollars.

The second chief is Geodol—called in English Noel Jeddore—who represented Olibia in his absence. Geodol is the owner of one of the two cows on the Reservation, and his brother possesses the second one. The Chieftainship is not hereditary, but is conferred, when a vacancy occurs, on the man the people prefer. They are easy to govern and seldom quarrel. They have no intoxicating liquor and seldom obtain any. They pay 60 to 70 cents a pound for their tobacco, 20 to 30 cents for gunpowder, and 10 cents for shot. They sell their fur locally where they make their small family purchases.

The head of each family has his own special trapping ground in the interior, over which others may travel, fish, or shoot, but not trap. For example Geodol, the second Chief, traps about Gulp Lake; Olibia, the chief, about Mount Sylvester; Nicholas Jeddore about Burnt Hill; George Jeddore at Bare Hill and Middle Ridge; Stephen Jeddore at Scaffold Hill; Noel Matthews at Great Burnt Lake; &c.

> None go as far north as the railway, but Meiklejohn goes as far as John's Pond. Europeans are encroaching on their trapping lands, but do not go far inland. This pushes the Micmacs further inland to get away from the Europeans. They claim no fishing rights at sea, and say frankly they are only trappers and guides.
>
> They go inland in September, when their first care is to shoot a deer and smoke the flesh as food. They return home from the 20th to the 25th November to prepare their traps for fox, lynx, otter, and bear. In December they shoot, as winter food for the family, does and young stags, but not old stags. They say the arctic hare is now very rare on their trapping lands; and snipe, geese, and ducks are far fewer than they were a few years ago. They appear to be very careful not to waste venison, never killing any deer they do not actually require and use as food.
>
> It is not possible to regard the present condition and the prospects of this settlement of Micmacs as being bright. Game, their principal food, is manifestly becoming more difficult to procure; their trapping lands are being encroached upon by Europeans; they are not seamen; they are not fishermen; and they do not understand agriculture. In the middle of their Reservation a saw-mill has been in operation some years, apparently on the allotment of Bernard John, but without his sanction or permission, and, it seems, in spite of the protests of the community. None of the Micmacs work at this mill. Formerly they cut logs for it, but the trees that grew near the water have, they say, all been used up and there are none left within their reach that they could bring to the water. The saw-mill is thus an eyesore to them, as it is on what they regard as their land, in defiance of them.[13]

With respect to the reservation, he suggested that, despite its failure to fulfil the licence conditions, his government should not withhold grants from families "as a matter of grace, if only they applied for them and could show how they could use the land."

> It would not be difficult to find a location for the community that would be more suitable for them as far as cultivation is concerned, and be equally good for hunting and trapping. With some aid, such as supplies of seed potatoes and a few animals, they could no doubt derive much greater resources than at present from agriculture, especially if to that were added a good school for the young.[14]

MacGregor did not specify an alternative site nor did government pursue relocation.

MacGregor promoted agriculture to uplift the Micmac. He spoke sympathetically on another issue; namely, dependence on the interior and its resources:

> The question of their trapping lands will have to be dealt with before long. Each man regards his rights to his trapping area as unimpeachable. They are recognised at present among themselves, but they have no official sanction for their trapping lands either as a community or as individuals, just as they have no official title to the Reservation.[15]

He recommended official sanction, in reality a formal recognition of Indian rights.

Concluding his report he again recognized Micmac rights:

> . . . as an ethnic unit . . . the Micmac community, such as it is, will not, at least for several generations, be absorbed into the European population of Newfoundland. It is at present a separate entity, and as such clearly requires special attention and treatment at the hands of the Administration, for the reservation families have claims on Newfoundland by right of a century of Micmac occupation; and by virtue of the European blood that probably each one of them has inherited.[16]

This advice was ignored and Indian rights remained in limbo. The government failed to secure Indian land. This neglect facilitated further erosion of Micmac culture.

MacGregor suggested that Micmac ethnicity no longer existed. Yet his references to St. Anne, the Chief and the family trapping territory shows there was a distinct Micmac culture. Later this culture, already under pressure, would be attacked from an unexpected quarter, the church.

NOTES

1. English authorities first learned of the timber resources in Bay d'Espoir through Captain Taverner's report on his survey of 1714 in which he spoke of the "abundance of timber which affords plenty of . . . masts for ships, very good Timber of all sorts. . . ." CO 194/4/444. They were reminded by Captain Cook in 1766 and his survey report referring to the "Great Plenty of all Sorts of Wood, common to this country. . . ." James Cook, *Directions for Navigating on Part of the South Coast of Newfoundland*, (London: James Cook, 1766), p. 18. For a brief historical account of the seasonal logging industry in Bay d'Espoir during the 19th century, see Edward Cokes, "The Spatial Patterns of Log cutting in Bay d'Espoir, 1895-1922,"

Unpublished MA Thesis, Memorial University of Newfoundland, 1973.

2. Tocque, *Newfoundland as it Was*, pp. 200-201.
3. Rev. M. F. Howley, *Ecclesiastical History of Newfoundland* (Boston: Doyle and Whittle, 1888), pp. 319-321.
4. Gordon Perry, ''Old and Interesting Book,'' *Holy Cross Annual*, 2nd Edition, 1951-52.
5. PANL, Census, 1845.
6. Captain John Parish, ''Abstract of Account of the Fisheries between the 5th June and 22nd August,'' *JLC*, 1869, p. 26.
7. Captain Malcolm, ''Report of Captain Malcolm, of H.M.S. *Danae*, of Fisheries on the South West Coast of Newfoundland, visited between 3rd and 15th (inclusive), of June.'' *JLC*, 1872, p. 177.
8. Cokes, ''Spatial Patterns,'' p. 33.
9. Ibid., p. 32.
10. CO 194/273/145-159. Micmac Indians at Bay d'Espoir, Report on Settlement, 1908, by Governor William MacGregor.
11. Ibid., p. 148.
12. Ibid., p.148.
13. Ibid., pp. 147-154.
14. Ibid., p. 154.
15. Ibid., p. 155.
16. Ibid., p. 157.

CHAPTER 8

Land tenure — Family hunting territories — Speck and Millais lists — Workings of the system

Every society organizes its subsistence activities to include a system of land tenure as a means of controlling harvests. By custom certain individuals or groups are granted rights of access to or control over resources. Whatever its specific form, the system must ensure fair distribution and management of key resources.[1]

The aboriginal Micmac held land in common. A communal form of tenure was essential considering that major game animals are migratory. It was necessary that everyone be free to hunt. If this freedom were restricted by individuals or families, people would either prosper or perish depending on the availability of localized game. At inland camps families banded together to hunt; sharing meat ensured equitable distribution.

This system collapsed under the pressures of the fur trade.[2] With game depleted and families bound by trade, there evolved a new form of land tenure, the family hunting territory system.

The importance of small game to the fur trade presented different circumstances from those of the prehistoric period. Beaver, otter, fox and marten could not support the traditional unit, and there was no need for a cooperative hunt. Small family groups could harvest fur as efficiently as the larger group. The species concerned are relatively stationary, so the rule of common tenure, of free access to all land, no longer applied. Individual families would trap in a relatively confined area.

This is effective management when families take care to conserve game stocks, and neighbours agree not to impose. When conceded an exclusive right to take fur, a family was assured reliable harvests over the long term.

> If the right to take furs were not exclusive, the future returns that would accrue from an individual's conservation efforts would not be fully appropriable to himself, his experienced rate of return on investments in maintaining the beaver population (and others) would fall by a proportion equal to the share in the total returns that he expected to be captured by others, and less investment would be undertaken than if the right were exclusive.[3]

If communal access were retained, the efforts of individuals to conserve would be of no personal benefit since others would be free to take what they chose to leave.

The basic feature of the territory is the sole and exclusive right to trap within the area. Tenure by territory does not involve ownership of land but rather gives a priority of access. Territorial rights do not bear directly upon the land, but on its resources.

The family territory system is a method of wildlife management. It was adopted by the Micmac of Nova Scotia and other tribes as the fur trade spread.[4] With the expansion of tribal territory to Newfoundland the system was similarly applied.

Speck was interested in hunting territories. He produced a map outlining the division of territories (see below) within the Newfoundland interior, 13 in all, each referred to as *ntuylwo.mi*, ''my hunting ground.''[5]

	Proprietor's Name	**District**
1	Little Jim John	Grandys brook and King George IV lake to high barrens near coast.
2	Paul Benoit (and sons)	White Bear river to Round pond, Bay du Nord.
3	George Jeddore	Bay d'Espoir to Belle Bay and inland.
4	Louis John	About Long Harbour river north to Terra Nova river.
5	Louis Morris (hereditary chieftain)	Gander river to Gander lake and Gambo.
6 6a	John Paul (originally Tom Joe)	Narrow strip from Hall's bay up Badger's brook into interior.
7	John Matthews	Noel Paul's brook to Meelpaeg Lake.
8	Frank Joe	Sandy lake through Red Indian and Victoria lakes.
9	Ben Paul	Deer lake through Grand lake to Lloyd's pond.
10	John Stevens	Humber river to coast.
11	Steven Stevens	Humber river to Hall's bay.
12	Beaton family	Recent general tracts about lower Exploits river.
13	Mathew Mitchell (old chieftain family)	King George IV lake, elsewhere at will.[6]

Speck's map probably represents the status of Micmac in the 19th century, rather than in 1914. (For example #5, ''Louis Morris''—the Maurice Louis already mentioned—died in 1880.) Territories of families he did not meet or who were not known to his informants were omitted: Charles Francis of Gander Bay, John Barrington of Piper's Hole River and the Johns of Glenwood, to name a few.

A list of Micmac hunters and their respective territories (see next page) was compiled by J. G. Millais. All those listed save Frank Joe, John Barrington, the Pauls and the Michels were from Conne River.

Millais lists 18 contiguous territories from Grey River to Terra Nova and Piper's Hole River. Territories often paralleled a particular drainage system or section of it. Family names were associated with ponds and river systems. ''Western Maelpeg, that's Grey River water, Noel Louis' country; the Strides, they belong to Big River water,'' a hunter might explain.

Territorial boundaries were not rigidly defined and tended to move somewhat over time. Trapping is an extensive form of land use. A family would cover their territory completely over a season or two and rarely would work outlying areas of uncertain status where neighbouring families might have rights.

Virgin country or unused land was open. Evidence of occupation was understood as prior claim and accepted. If the country appeared unoccupied the hunter set traps or snares, establishing a claim:

> I remember one fall me and my father were out furring. We circled down around Mount Sylvester towards Diamond Lake. That was John country, or was at one time, but we didn't see no sign so we set our snares. When we came back a few days later we found our snares struck up. Uncle Steve had come by while we were gone and hung them up. That was his right so we didn't trap there no more.

The proprietor, Steve John, who had not worked this portion of his territory for some time, felt that ''he belonged to that country.'' By striking up the snares, he left clear evidence of his decision, one which Joe Hinx accepted.

Trapping, a relatively individualized activity, involves an obligation to be mindful of one's neighbours. Steve John could have respected Hinx's claim. As Hinx explains, if he found an animal

Proprietor's Name	District
Frank Joe	Burgeo country and Western Maelpeg.
Little Frank Benoit	Spruce Pond, NW of Maelpeg.
Paul Benoit	Crooked Lake.
Frank Benoit	Crooked Lake.
Ned Pullet	Long Pond, between two W. Maelpegs.
Noel Louis	Western Maelpeg.
John Benoit	Nimooch-we-godie.
Frank MacDonald	Godoleik (W. of Conn).
Ben Benoit	Island Pond, NW of W. Maelpeg.
Noel Matthews Martin and Michael	Crooked Lake.
Noel Jeddore John Denny Jeddore	Sandy Pond.
Stephen Joe (stepbrother of Joe J.)	Burnt Hill and Podopekgutch.
Joe Jeddore	Burnt Hill and Upper Gander.
Nicholas Jeddore	Burnt Hill and Upper Gander.
John Bernard	Middle Ridge and Glenwood.
John Stride	Northern side of Sylvester.
Reuben Lewis	Kagudeck.
Stephen Bernard	Sandy Pond and Shoe Hill Ridge.
Peter John Mickey John	Eastern Maelpeg.
Mickey John Peter John	St. John's Pond.
John Hinx, Paddy Hinx, Johnny Hinx	Wiskomonagodie, Eastern Partridge-berry Hills, S. of Maelpeg.
Mathew Burke Johnny Benoit	Tolt and Piper's Hill Brook.
John Barrington	Eastern side of Tolt.
Lewis John	Eastern side of Tolt.
Len Joe	Grand Lake.
Ben, Abraham and Noel Paul	Exploits River.
Matty Michel and son	Bonne Bay.[7]

trapped in one of those snares, he would "give buddy a second chance" by hanging up the animal and resetting the snare:

> If I comes on another man's territory, probably I comes across his trap, fox into it. I kill that fox and hang it up where it was to. If I thought that man wasn't going to come round for it to spoil, I'd clean it for him.

MacGregor was informed that hunters were forbidden to trap in a neighbour's territory, but everyone was free to travel, fish or hunt wherever they pleased. Tenure by territory imposes an exclusive right of access to fur-bearing animals only. This results from a dependence upon caribou, the most nomadic of big game animals. The chance of abundance or scarcity within any family's territory meant that hunters were allowed to hunt in neighbouring territory.

A more explicit rule against trespass was invoked in Cape Breton, where moose, almost sedentary in winter, was the game animal. Moose were covered by the same exclusive right of access extended to fur-bearing animals and were subject to the same conservation strategy. Trespass, while not strictly forbidden, was not encouraged. A hunter would be reluctant to venture onto a neighbour's territory and did so only when necessary.

The Micmac paid careful attention to prey population and distribution. Each family acted as a wildlife management team. For example, rather than taking a modest harvest from the entire territory, as might seem wise, families might instead concentrate their efforts within a smaller area for two or three seasons, trapping almost to the point of exhaustion. This method assured a continuous turnover since stocks in those 'overtrapped' areas could be replenished by immigrant animals. Even when taking a modest harvest one could never be certain of leaving a breeding pair in each lodge. Trappers "fertilized" or baited their country. On spring caribou hunts they left portions of the carcass. A vixen, for example, pregnant since February and now almost due, would be apt to den near the food. Thus the hunter returning the next fall could expect to find a family of fox or lynx.

Fur trapping rights were retained by the family, passing from father to son. The territory was not divided on succession; the sons shared a common interest. Micmac trappers seldom worked in teams of more than two or three; the eldest and presumably most experienced son was acknowledged as the leader.

Trapping teams were kinship based, with brothers or fathers and sons working together. Convenience produced other partnerships. Bachelors and only sons often looked to other families for partners. Steve Bernard, sole survivor of Joe Bernard, trapped with Mickey John from a neighbouring territory. In this partnership the resident trapper, Steve, was the leader. Fur was shared equally. "It didn't make any difference to us, sharing the wealth, whatever we caught," explains Larry Paul.

If a territory was not producing a neighbour might suggest a trapper work with him. A man might suggest a partnership out of respect, a desire to learn or an interest in the country. A Paul from Bay St. George joined the Stride family of Conne River for several years. Paul invited three Stride brothers to trap in his territory before establishing their own. Orphaned and illegitimate children were granted territory through adoption, often taking the family name as well.

Tenure remained valid only as long as the family worked their territory. Virgin country was fair game, and as Sylvester Jeddore advises, "you would never let the country go to waste." Abandoned territory was quickly absorbed by a neighbouring family. The Johns took over Bernard country when Steve and his family moved to Bishop's Falls. When a territory was temporarily neglected, perhaps because of sickness, others moved in for the duration. The proprietor encouraged this, ensuring that his camps and gear would be kept in good repair.

The Micmac blazed trees to mark overland trails and kept "country paths" clear. Where possible, they cleared boulders from rough sections of rivers to lessen the risk of capsizing and built rock cairns on the barrens to serve as direction markers. Some used a distinctive mark, a particular blaze or type of cairn.

The family territory system was the foundation of Micmac subsistence. MacGregor noted that the territorial rights of families were respected without question. Millais remarked:

> The sanctity of their trapping-grounds is considered inviolate by the Micmac. They live on fairly good terms with the Newfoundlanders, but let another Indian or a white man come into their trapping area for the purpose of taking fur, and the amiable red man is at once transformed into a demon of rage and jealousy.

Under tribal law disputes over territorial rights were arbitrated by the Chief, yet there is no record or recollection of any dispute.

If the Micmac recognized the sanctity of their trapping grounds, the government and Newfoundlanders clearly did not. Conne River territories remained stable through most of the 19th century. Eventually they were pressured from the south and north. Settlers in Bay d'Espoir occupied the lower Salmon River to Long Pond and the lower reaches of other streams emptying into the bay. Settlers pushed up the Bay du Nord, Long Harbour, Terra Nova and Northwest Gander rivers.

The Micmac were resentful and asserted their rights. While out checking his trapline Mickey John came on the tracks of three settlers. John found his snares cut and his pelts taken. Furious, he followed the thieves, catching up with them at Long Harbour River. He demanded his pelts. At first they refused, but eventually they relented.

Millais recounts a similar story involving Joe Jeddore:

> I only saw Joe angry on one occasion, and that was when we were descending a rocky hill to the Gander, some distance above Rolling Fall, when we found two lynx traps made during the previous winter. Joe's eyes blazed, and he gave a grunt of dissatisfaction. When he got to camp he put down my rifle carefully and disappeared into the woods, returning some ten minutes afterwards with a face of thunder and lightning.
>
> "It is as I thought," he hissed, "they have killed *my* beavers, and I will get even with the devils," only he did not say devils. Then he proceeded to let loose his passion on the white trappers who had for the first time ascended the Gander, a province which Joe considered his exclusive right, and poured such a torrent of threats and abuse on their heads that I have seldom heard. . . .

Traditional ways changed in the 20th century. The relationship the Micmac had with the land was compromised as families left trapping and subsistance hunting for guiding and logging.

NOTES

1. For an account of Indian land tenure, see Harold E. Driver, *Indians of North America* (Chicago: University of Chicago Press, 1961), pp. 246-261.
2. For an analysis of the various disruptive influences imposed by the development of the fur trade among the Micmac, see Hoffman, "Historical Ethnography," pp. 218-236.

3. John McManus, ''An Economic Analysis of Indian Behavior in the North American Fur Trade,'' *Journal of Economic History*, vol. XXXII, 1972, pp 36-53.
4. Perhaps the earliest mention of the institution of the family territory was recorded by Fr. Chrestien Le Clercq in the 1670s.
5. Speck, *Beothuk and Micmac*, p. 130.
6. Ibid., pp. 132-134.
7. Millais, *Untrodden Ways*, p. 222.

CHAPTER 9

Season on the country — Hunting and trapping — Material culture (skin and birchbark canoes, snowshoes, sleds, wigwams and clothing)

The "season on the country" for the trappers of Conne River began in late August or early September. Teams made an initial trip to the family territories. Supplies (flour, sugar, tea, perhaps some pork, snare wire, axe, rifle, ammunition, cooking gear and new traps) were carried in a bedroll or "bundle" of canvas or caribou hide rolled up and cinched with a pack strap, *wskubuksn*. It was tied so that two loops were free, one to go across the chest, the other over the head. Loads of over 100 pounds were common.

Bound for the east country they hiked a well-beaten track across Little River to Meddonagonix; those of the west crossed the bay then followed a trail to Long Pond. Two or three days later they would be settled at their main tilt.

First they hunted caribou and black bear, laying up a supply of meat and fat. The southern caribou herd moving onto open country was easily spotted browsing in small herds or companies. Taking caribou under these conditions required skill. Most tried to approach to 50 yards, to ensure a clean kill. On barrens with little or no cover the trick was to identify the lead animal, usually an older doe, and observe her movements. Anticipating her, hunters circled to position themselves where the caribou would come in range. They stalked, crawling on all fours, moving slowly, sometimes using a spruce bough as camouflage. In a small open space, a pair of hunters would organize a flush with one circling around to drive the herd towards the other.

On the first caribou hunt they concentrated on larger stags, favoured for the quantity of meat, for curing over an open fire of spruce boughs until hard and dry. Cured meat was eaten dry or boiled. Stag hides were also preferred for canoes, clothing, bedding, snowshoes and skin boots, the standard country footwear.

By late September, with mating season approaching, stags could be "tolled" within range. Millais saw Joe Jeddore tolling a stag using:

> . . . an appalling series of loud grunts, enough, as I thought, to scare every deer out of the country but not so our amorous friend,

> who at once replied with similar noises, and trotted up to within 150 yards.[1]

Stag hunting was abandoned with the onset of the rut. Changes in body chemistry rendered their meat "so foul even my dogs won't touch it," as Walter John remarked. Younger stags, unaffected and unattached, could be safely shot. If additional meat was required during the rut hunters sought solitary animals unattached to a harem.

The Micmac took what was needed and wasted little. The meat was cured. The rib cage was sometimes cooked whole, mounted over a fire or left under a tin stove. When cooked the ribs were withdrawn and the slab of meat rolled and packed. The head was roasted, suspended over an open fire or boiled in a large pot. The resulting combination of flesh, fat and brain assumed a texture like tinned corned beef when cooled. Entrails were eaten; intestines were flushed and plaited. After a kill hunters often indulged in a "gut feed," boiling intestines with liver, heart and lungs. Hip and leg bones were broken into short lengths and boiled until the fat melted. The marrow was removed and either eaten alone or mixed with fat. "I give you a taste of it and I'll have to drive you off with my gun," advises Peter Oliver of Bay St. George. "We didn't waste anything, never threw anything away, except maybe for the feet. Even then some of us used to eat them too, like the pig's feet you can buy in the stores today."

Black bears were hunted as they fed on ripe berries on the barrens and rocky hillsides. Bear fat was rendered in a large pot. Sometimes caribou fat was added to produce a firmer texture. Blood and other impurities were skimmed off and the melted fat was poured into birchbark vessels and left to cool overnight. The rendered fat, *muinomi*, was used as cooking oil and butter. In fall a prime bear yielded considerable fat, enough to fill a large flour sack in some cases.

Bear meat was eaten fresh or preserved either by smoking or boiling in salted water. Cormack learned bear meat was "by many of the Indians esteemed next to that of the beaver's, and it has the peculiar quality of not clogging the stomach, however much of it is eaten."[2] Organs and entrails were eaten as a matter of taste. One old hunter, Noel Louis, used bear stomach in a unique fashion. It was turned inside out, stuffed with caribou or beaver, sewn tight and boiled for several hours. The stomach, if properly sewn, would preserve the stuffing for some time.

Considering the number of bears hunted and the savage character of a wounded bear, it is remarkable that no hunter was killed. Reuben Louis, the chief, was

> . . . hunting some ten years ago with Noel Jeddore near Burnt Hill. Reuben fired at a large dog bear, and badly wounded it. After tracking for a short distance they saw the bear lying still, and Reuben went up to it, and gave it a kick to see if life was extinct; the bear, which was far from being dead, sprang up and seized the hunter by one leg, at the same time flinging his gun out of reach. Reuben lay as still as he could, but the bear chawed up both his legs and one hand, whilst Noel ran round trying to fire, but fearful of wounding his friend. At last Noel came so near that the bear dropped Reuben a second to growl at him, and whilst doing so he obtained a shot and dropped the bear dead. After some weeks in camp Reuben walked out to the coast and had completely recovered in three months.[3]

Black bears can cause considerable mischief. One of Millais' guides was victimized by bears:

> Steve Bernard carried a sack of flour and all his stores and ammunition to his log tilt on Jubilee Lake in the autumn of 1902, and then repaired to the coast to see the priest. When he returned the whole tilt, including fir logs weighing several hundred pounds, were scattered through the woods, and not a dollar's worth of the outfit remained.[4]

The bear-proof box, *lscotegan*, constructed of logs, was six feet square and flat roofed, built between two large and well-rooted evergreens. A hole was chopped through each tree at the height of the box. A sturdy pole was run through these holes and wedged holding the roof secure. The only way a bear could gain entry was to uproot one of the trees.

Bears were trapped with a snare, the looped end suspended from a sturdy tree branch over a setting of bait. A partial enclosure of logs and boughs ensured the proper approach. A thick heavy log with a hole chipped through the upper end leaned against the branch. The anchor end of the snare wire was run through this hole, then secured to the branch. Once the bear was snared and struggling, the log would shake free and fall, tightening the noose.

Trapping began in earnest in mid-October, after all necessary preparations had been made—*lscotegan*, skin boots, and caches of dried meat were all ready. Metal traps were prepared, and snare wire was cut into lengths and smoked over a fire of green boughs to mask the brassy colour and smell. Traps, either hung from trees or submersed in a pond, were retrieved, cleaned and restored to proper function.

Beaver and otter in peak fall condition were taken by firearms as well as traps. Cormack explains:

> Before sunset the hunter posts himself undiscovered as near as possible to the leeward side of their house; the beavers at that time come out, one following another. Directly any of their heads appear above the water, it is fired at either with ball or shot, and sometimes a whole family is thus killed in succession. If any escape, their return to their house is watched before sunrise next morning, in like manner as their departure was in the evening. Their bodies float to the shore.[5]

The body would float if the beaver had been feeding previously; freshly ingested browse added buoyancy. A beaver could be lured from its house by sabotaging its dam. Beaver could be tolled close to shore with a variety of sounds. Millais was told, "a hissing noise, or one produced by munching the lips" and "a sound made by tapping the trousers with the hand" would attract them. Best of all was "a sound that resembled the cutting of chips off a tree. It is said that the unfortunate rodents never fail to respond to this noise."[6] Camouflaged traps, scented with the beaver's castor gland, were set along feeding trails. Alternatively, traps were tied to a frame of boughs, then anchored underwater at the lodge entrance.

Otters were hunted, trapped and sometimes tolled with a shrill whistle. Given their nervous, attentive nature, always quick to notice any disturbance, one had to be particularly discreet. To anchor a trap on their overland trails, the hunter would select a dry bleached stick rather than cut a new one. The bright scar of a fresh cut was sure to catch the otter's eye. When trapping at their rubs, a pair of long poles was laid in a funnel shape to direct their descent. These would be left in place for a full season, allowing the otter to become accustomed to the disturbance, before the hunter set a trap below the mouth of the funnel.

The gravity-weighted trap, or deadfall, was sometimes used. Effective and easily constructed from local materials, it saved packing heavy traps about the country. By the turn of the century it was supplanted but not entirely replaced by the steel trap.

The men also pursued long-haired animals, principally fox and lynx, both taken by snare. A pair of hunters might strew the country with as many as 500 snares over the course of a season. Fox were taken where they followed caribou leads through the bush or on the open country where they fed on berries. Being shy of water both the fox and the lynx could be snared on fallen trees used as bridges across a brook. If no deadfall were handy the men felled a tree. Both species were taken with baited traps as well. A trap baited with trout or caribou buried in a shallow hole would catch a fox as it dug to investigate the tempting odour. Hares were the common bait for lynx. Fox and lynx were tolled with the mimicked scream of a stricken hare.

Throughout the fall and early winter teams scoured their territories for fur. Wherever possible they travelled by canoe, scouting ponds and brooks for signs and occasionally branching off on foot to set lines of snares and traps. In some territories they constructed a series of three or four main camps laid out in a circle, each spaced one or two days' walk from the next. By stages they would work this circuit often laying branch lines. It was important to keep a close watch on gear for there were scavengers. Everything caught was taken to camp for preparation. Fox, otter, and lynx pelts were stretched inside out over a mould for cleaning while that of the beaver was stretched flat and tacked on a frame. Fat and "vellum" were scraped off using a knife. The value of the pelt depended as much on the quality of preparation as on its size or texture.

This work was done in camp, preferably on bad-weather days. The pelts prepared and gear reset, the men hunted geese and ducks, black ducks especially. Hares were snared, trout and ouananiche caught for food and bait. This was a high-protein diet, with various soups, stews and roasts providing essential nutrients.

By late November, or December, migratory caribou would finally hit the southern interior after their trek from the north. In the "west country," teams often timed their return trip to coincide with this migration. If there was a heavy snowfall the caribou would break trail. Trappers of the "east country" would also make one final hunt on this return trip, again packing out fresh meat for families and friends. Some meat would be left behind as insurance against poor hunting later. Carcasses, whole or quartered, were hung up to freeze or were buried in snow. Where trails converged as they approached Conne River, incoming teams left spare flour, fat and meat on a scaffold for the benefit of later comers.

The hunter's season on the country did not end as hunting and trapping continued through the winter. Now there was Christmas to celebrate, trade to be done, friends to visit and firewood to gather. Time at home was spent repairing snowshoes and sleds, and producing various handicrafts for trade and home use. Country travel was governed by snow conditions. Deep fresh snow was impossible to travel by dogteam or snowshoe. Trips would await a mild spell followed by a cold snap to settle the snow under a firm crust. In the meantime they snared rabbits, took partridge and speared eels through the ice.

The winter snows settled firmly into a solid crust by late February or early March—time for serious hunting. Millais described a collective hunt, which he called a "surround."

> The Indians depart at daybreak, and after locating a herd of several hundreds in a valley they occupy all the main trails leading out of it, and send some one to move the deer. As soon as they are started the caribou rush for the passes, where the Indians lie concealed, and a considerable number are killed at short range with guns loaded with swan-shot.[7]

The harvest was shared freely when hunting as a group. They feasted on the delicacies, and loaded their sleds with quartered caribou to take home. Liver, tongue, and other favourites were shared with elderly and inactive members of the village.

The men returned by dogteam to family territories in early spring, not to trap, for pelts were now past their prime, but to prepare for the next season. They took this opportunity to pack in supplies. Camps damaged by wind or snow were repaired. Canoes left at freeze-up were returned to their proper stash. Again they took caribou. The herds which had wintered in the southern interior began the trek northward and could be intercepted along their leads. It was here that the hunters left bait for fox and lynx.

Following breakup they went "ratting," to trap muskrats and otter. Unlike other species, the muskrat retains its prime pelt into spring. Travelling by canoe, the men shot and trapped muskrat, often in considerable numbers.

Salmon gathered along the inshore waters of Conne Arm before ascending Conne Brook. The Micmac speared them, eels and brook trout from torchlit canoes. Smolt or tidewater salmon were trapped in weirs, fences of wooden stakes across the mouth of the brook. Gates were left open while the tide rose, admitting the smolt, then closed, trapping the fish. Similar traps built upstream across a narrow stretch of river were fitted with a bag net.

Families camped at river mouths for the salmon season. The harvest was not governed by specialized tenure. A particular family might become associated with a stretch of river, however this did not involve the proprietary rights associated with trapping territories. The salmon harvest was often collective, with two or more families working together. Salmon and eels were eaten fresh, smoked or dried.

The mouth of Little River, a mile around the eastern shore of the bay, was another favourite summer campsite. Though its salmon run was smaller than Conne Brook, the site was renowned for trout, blueberries, bakeapples and partridgeberries.

* * * * *

The aboriginal material culture of the Micmac is long lost.* The introduction of European technology meant skills used in the working of bone, wood and stone lost practical value and were abandoned. The Micmac adopted items that were an improvement over their own; at the same time they retained practical and effective old skills. Cultural borrowing worked both ways, as Europeans adopted various Micmac crafts and skills, particularly the canoe, snowshoe and sled.

The birchbark canoe was the principal means of water travel. Observers from the 16th to the 19th centuries from Gaspé to Newfoundland have established its universality. With the exception of the raised gunnel, the style of the Micmac canoe varied little from the standard model of northeastern tribes. A single sheet of birch bark was moulded to a ribbed and slatted frame. The bark was sewn to the frame with split roots and was waterproofed with fir gum. The result was a remarkably sturdy yet light craft.[8]

Conne River elders recall their fathers and grandfathers making birch bark canoes; they and Alexander Murray refer to an area near Long Pond where large birch was obtained.[9] In Newfoundland the

---

*See Ruth Whitehead, *Elitekey: Micmac Material Culture from 1600AD to the Present* (Halifax: Nova Scotia Museum, 1980).

"skin boat," the caribou-hide canoe, predominated throughout the 19th and early 20th centuries, the preference being determined by the abundance of caribou and the scarcity of large birch. Also, as Speck was told, the skin boat was "more convenient on the portages and more quickly made."[10] Cormack described James John's craft:

> It was made of wicker-work, covered over outside with deer skins sewed together and stretched on it, nearly of the usual form of canoes, with a bar or beam across the middle, and one on each end to strengthen it. The skin covering, flesh side out, was fastened or laced to the gunwales, with thongs of the same material. Owing to decay and wear it requires to be renewed once in from six to twelve weeks. It is these temporary barks that the Indians of Newfoundland of the present day [use to] navigate the lakes and rivers of the interior.[11]

Canoes averaged between 10 and 12 feet in length, using two large stag hides. These were sewn end-to-end with sinew from the caribou's spine and stretched over the frame with the head portion of the hides hooked over the prow and stern. Three or four hides were used for larger craft; added sections were trimmed rectangular and sewn to the middle. Roots or hide was used to secure the hide to the gunnels; caribou fat was the waterproofing.

The skin boat was not as durable as the birchbark canoe, but its construction was simpler. Hides punctured or worn through were patched and waterproofed easily. One veteran hunter recalls his father "patching" their canoe in midstream by plugging the puncture with a piece of cured caribou meat which expanded and stemmed the flow. The skin boat was buoyant and portable; on a long portage hunters removed the frame and packed the hide. A new frame was made in short order.

In later years the use of bark and hide canoes was abandoned in favour of canvas-covered models. The Micmac duplicated the design of examples brought by sportsmen.

Snowshoes and dogsleds are distinctly native. The Newfoundland Micmac term for snowshoes is "rackets," from the French, *la raquette*. The construction is familiar: an elongated teardrop hardwood frame bound at the rear and reinforced with two crosspieces. Commonly they were made of yellow birch, or witch hazel, a strong, fine-grained pliable wood. For the meshing, long strips of caribou hide, preferably the thinner hide from a stag's underbelly, were cut into two thicknesses. The thinner strips were used for the toe and heel sections, the thicker for the centre portion. Snowshoe size varied to suit the prevailing snow conditions: larger for travel over loose powder, smaller for crusted snow.

The Micmac employed sleds on crust snow. The following description of sled construction, confirmed by contemporary tribesmen, we have from a 19th century sportsman:

> A hunting toboggan is six feet long, composed of two side pieces of spruce, six inches wide, and one inch in thickness, rounded off in front, and square behind; these are placed parallel to each other, at the distance of two feet, and joined at the upper sides by wooden benches of maple or other hardwood. Strips of thin sheet iron, two inches wide, and turned up in front to serve as runners, are then nailed or screwed to the bottom of the side pieces. Thin pieces of wood are placed over the benches, on the top of which the load is fastened by rope, or thongs of hide. . . . In lieu of iron runners cedar may be used, turned up at the ends. Iron runners are better in a thaw, and wooden when the snow is dry. A rope, or better still, a "lugging strap," is made fast to each side of the foremost benches, the centre of the strap is then put across the chest, and placing your hands behind, you grasp it with a twist, which gives additional purchase. In this manner a man can haul a couple of hundred weight.[12]

The toboggan is a sled, *tepaqn*, as opposed to the familiar child's toboggan, *tepaqnapsku'l.* The sled with runners was preferred, although both were made by the aboriginal Micmac. This account describes it as a hand-hauled vehicle. Teams of one to three dogs were an innovation introduced by the Montagnais.

The traditional Micmac shelter was the wigwam, a conical structure of timber and birchbark.[13] The design was common to all Algonquian tribes. A level area was cleared and the superstructure erected. Four poles, *pɨsi'k*, of spruce or fir about 14 feet long, were bound at the top with spruce roots. Smaller poles were interspersed and tied with roots. Broad strips of bark were wrapped around the frame with successive strips overlapping those below. These were sewn with roots. A second siding of poles packed with moss was laid against the bark to shed rain and resist wind. Mats of woven grass or reeds were sometimes used more lining. The entrance, framed by sticks bound to the *pɨsi'k*, was covered by a flap of caribou hide hinged on top and weighted below with two sticks sewn to the hide.

The floor was covered with a soft carpet of evergreen boughs, then caribou blankets. Cooking pots were suspended over a central fire. Smoke escaped through an aperture at the apex.

Wigwams varied in size depending on the length of the poles. Fleming noted a very large wigwam was built as a "house of prayer" whenever a number of families gathered. The wigwam, or at least its bark component, was transported when families moved. The poles, sticks and moss were replaced at a new campsite, but in some areas there was a scarcity of birch. The bark, gently heated to make it pliable, was rolled into bundles and packed.

In addition to the conical design, the Newfoundland Micmac also built rectangular log wigwams, similar to the frontier cabin, with the logs on the front and rear vertical rather than horizontal.[14] The Beothuk also built wigwams in this manner.[15]

The wigwam was the standard dwelling of the coast and the interior. As logging developed in Bay d'Espoir, they were replaced by "small and inferior" wooden frame houses, as MacGregor described them. Country wigwams gave way to log cabins or "tilts."

The Micmac erected temporary shelters on the country. "Side camps" were usually built for a single night. Cormack describes the procedure as demonstrated by Sylvester Joe:

> . . . about an hour before sunset a dry firm spot of ground on which to make a fire and to sleep under the thickest of the trees for shelter is pitched upon as near as possible to water, and an easy supply of wood for fuel. Care should be taken that the spot selected be not hollow underneath the moss that covers the ground, for in that case the fire, which always consumes its own bed, may sink before the night so far below the surface as to be useless, and expose a cavity amongst blocks of granite into which the firebrands have fallen, and sufficient to swallow up any slumberer that might chance to slide into it. Arms and knapsacks are then piled; as much wood is cut and brought to the spot as will serve to keep up a good fire all night. Tinder is made by pulverising a small piece of dry rotten wood and a little gunpowder together between the hands, and ignited by a spark from the lock of a pistol or fowling piece, or by any other means; the smoke of the fire affords instant relief from the constant devouring enemy, the flies. Boughs are broken from the surrounding spruce trees, two or three arms full to each person, to serve to lie and sleep on; they are laid on the ground at the windward side

> of the fire to be free from the smoke, tier upon tier, as feathers upon the back of a bird, the thick or broken ends placed in lines toward the fire, and form a kind of mat three or four inches in thickness. A few light poles are then cut and stuck in the ground along the windward side of the bed, inclined to an angle of about 45° over it toward the fire, on which to stretch a blanket to serve as a roof-screen in the event of rain during the night; the upper ends of the poles rest on a horizontal ridge pole, which is suspended at each end by a forked stick or a post. The camp being now ready for the general accommodation, wet clothes are taken off, and supper is prepared accordingly. The labour of exploring and hunting is such that the clothes are always wet from perspiration. A forked stick stuck in the ground is used for roasting by, and some pieces of rind of a birch or spruce tree serve for table cloth, platter, and torches. To make a camp after a day's hard fatigue required about an hour, and the whole should be done before it is dark.[16]

The roof screen was the canvas or caribou-hide rectangular sheet used to make the bundle.

Birch bark was used in a variety of crafts. It is a remarkably versatile material, light and pliable yet durable. It was stripped in thicknesses varying from that of onion skin to cardboard and could be cut, bent, folded and sewn in virtually any shape. Traditionally Micmac kitchen utensils were made from bark, including vessels used for boiling meat. These were replaced by metal pots, pans, and kettles. Some items persisted well into this century: drinking cups, *masquijo*, conical vessels for carrying water (*ula'qn*), and various bark boxes were commonly made on the country. A bone or metal awl was used to pierce holes through which split roots were threaded to sew the vessel. The Beothuk were known to make the same kind of vessels.[17] On the mainland these were often decorated with mosaic patterns of coloured porcupine quills.[18] This was done in Newfoundland using imported quills, as Speck found in 1914.[19]

The first traditional skill to succumb to the introduction of trade goods was the working of stone to produce axes and knives projectile points, which were quickly replaced with metal. In Newfoundland the only mention of stonework is Cormack's reference to the magnesium rocks used to make pipes at Pipestone Pond.[20]

Making clothes from caribou hide was another fading traditional skill when Speck visited:

> Children's coats were made from the skin of a caribou calf, with the eye-holes and ears left in place on the head, which fitted over the head of the child to form the hood. Often, when the hair was removed, the coats were decorated with checkerwork patterns and painted figures of animals. Pigments of red, yellow, brown, blue and black were prepared from various types of bark and berries.[21]

The skin boot, *mkɨsn*, was the standard country footwear until the second world war. Millais described how Steve Bernard and John Hinx made them:

> First of all the skin is cleaned, then Steve, making his knife sharp as a razor, shaved off all the hair. The two pair of boots were then cut into shape, and afterwards sewn tightly with a thread made from the sinews of the deer's back. A seamed-over stitch is used, and very tightly clinched. John Hinx was engaged meanwhile in making a deep trough out of a log of "var." In this he placed about an armful of "var" bark, carefully broken into fine pieces with the fingers. Boiling water was then poured into the trough, and the "boots" left to soak for twelve hours. After this they were taken out, well scraped, and put out to dry. They are then finished and perfectly soft, strong, and watertight.[22]

Tanning bark was removed from the roots of the tree rather than the trunk. The inner membrane, a juicy red, produced the colouring favoured by Micmac and Beothuk.

Skin boots rose above the knee and were tied with a leather thong. Boots were worked with fat, ideally otter fat, to make them waterproof. To ensure longer wear "shanks" were worn over skin boots. These were slippers made from the hide of the caribou's leg, cut and stitched so the knee joint fitted neatly over the heel. The cleaned and lightly salted hide was not tanned nor was the hair removed. Micmac on the west and northeast coasts used harp seal skin in making footwear.[23] In Bay d'Espoir, where such seals are nonexistent, caribou was used exclusively.

Caribou hair was commonly used in weaving before the introduction of sheep. The hair was combed from the hide and spun on a small wooden spindle. The loom was a wooden carved device with parallel bars anchored to a frame through which a series of holes was drilled. Speck described the method:

> When the woollen strands are ready to be woven, they are passed alternately through the holes and slits of the loom. One end of

> the group of gathered strands is tied to a post, or something equally convenient in the house, and the other end attached to the belt of the woman who is to do the weaving. Thus the loom is near the body of the weaver. By leaning backwards then the weaver can make the cords as tight as she desires. Without shuttle or bar the weaver then passes the ball of yarn with one hand between the alternate strands, separated vertically when the loom is raised with the other hand, and then back again when the loom is lowered. This produces an over-one under-one mesh, and the pattern is determined by the colors of the strands.[24]

Belts, garters and packstraps were woven. Rabbit wool was spun and woven for decorative bands for clothing.

NOTES

1. Millais, *Untrodden Ways*, p. 247.
2. Howley, *The Beothucks*, p. 154.
3. Millais, *Untrodden Ways*, pp. 223-224.
4. Ibid., pp. 95-96.
5. Howley, *The Beothucks*, p. 143.
6. Millais, *Untrodden Ways*, p. 211.
7. Ibid., p. 221.
8. For a detailed description of Micmac canoe design and construction, see Adney and Chapelle, *Bark Canoes and Skin Boats*, pp. 58-70.
9. Murray and Howley, *Geological Survey*, 1811, p. 625.
10. Speck, *Beothuk and Micmac*, p. 33.
11. Howley, *The Beothucks*, pp. 148-149.
12. Richard Lewes Dashwood, *Chiploquorgan or Life by the Camp Fire in Dominion of Canada and Newfoundland* (Dublin: Robert T. White, 1871), p. 101.
13. For a more detailed description, see Wallis and Wallis, *The Micmac Indians*, pp. 57-61.
14. Speck, *Beothuk and Micmac*, plates vii-viii.
15. Ibid., pp. 31-32.
16. Howley, *The Beothucks*, pp. 137-138.
17. Ibid., p. 76.
18. Ibid., p. 41.
19. Ibid., pp. 41-42.
20. Howley, *The Beothucks*, p. 146.
21. Speck, *Beothuk and Micmac*, p. 34.
22. Millais, *Untrodden Ways*, pp. 297-298.

23. Speck, *Beothuk and Micmac*, p. 36.
24. Ibid., pp. 37-38.

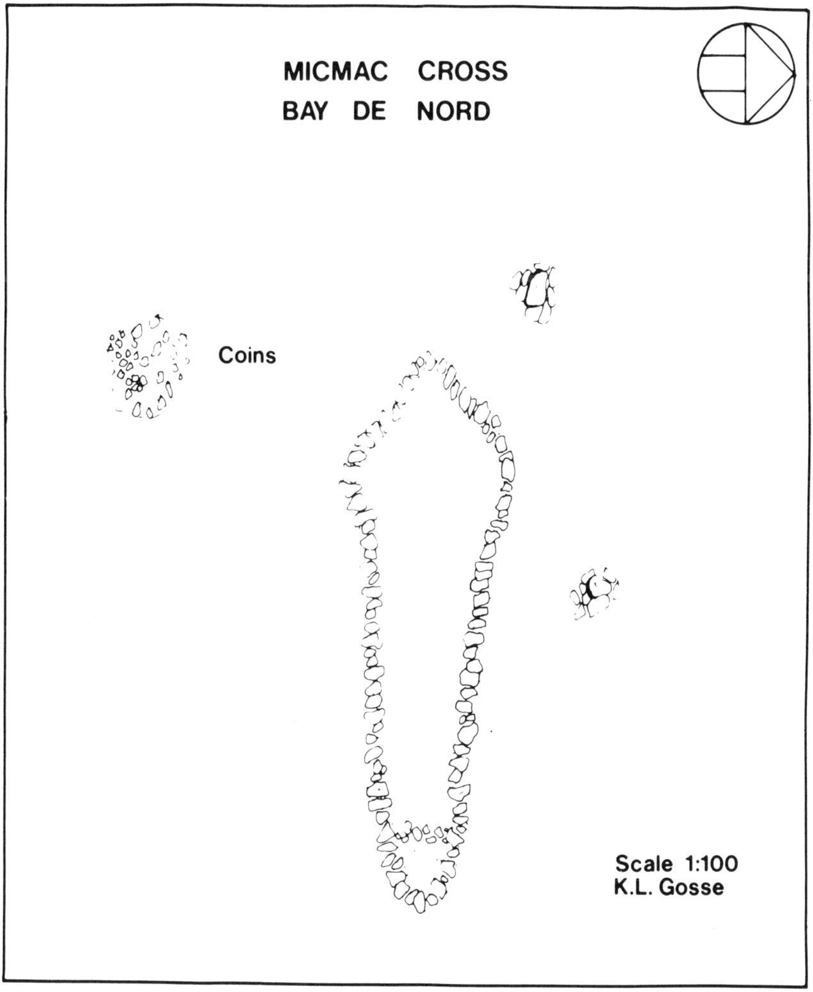

CHAPTER 10

Religion — Spiritualism — Bay de Nord Cross — St. Anne's Day — Burning of the 'junks' — Micmac hieroglyphics

Newfoundland Micmac are Roman Catholic, but in practice their faith is a synthesis of aboriginal and Christian elements.

> They are Roman Catholics, but their religious ceremonies, of which they are observant, consist of a combination of that church and their own primitive ceremonies blended together, to suit their convenience and tastes.[1]

Cormack did not elaborate on "primitive ceremonies," and little is known about prehistoric Micmac spiritualism. The earliest records of native life, mainly written by priests, were often biased. The Micmac believed in a creator, a soul, and an afterlife. This was natural spiritualism, a complex of spirits living within and controlling all life. Religious knowledge was embodied in the shaman. His *puion*, or supernatural power, allowed him to communicate with spirits who could affect the affairs of man.

In a study of Micmac shamanism Frederick Johnson visited a number of reserves in Nova Scotia. From elders he learned that the shaman could cause anything to happen through supernatural manipulation. He could inflict or cure sickness, foretell the future and divine the location of game. He was feared and respected. Johnson also learned that the shaman carried a leather pouch, *puoino'ti*, or *puoin* container, in which he kept small pieces of bone or stone. These *ntiomel* were animal spiritual helpers, each a messenger or agent who could, in the spirit world, do the shaman's bidding.

Johnson briefly visited Conne River in 1931 and found that Newfoundland Micmac were shamanistic. He "produced supplementary notes which were in no way different from information obtained on the mainland."[2] Speck had earlier noted shamanism when several hunters from Badger showed him their *ntiomel*. Shamanism and its underlying beliefs had waned by the time of Speck and Johnson. The shaman was condemned by priests as an agent of the devil. No one admitted that he was a shaman to Johnson and, while few recalled the belief and ritual, most acknowledged shamans and their "witching" powers.

Three examples of witching are recorded in Conne River. Micky John backpacked a load of prime fur to Gaultois. The clerk offered a low price, insisting he "wouldn't look at them for anything more." In that case, John replied, the clerk would not be able to see at all. The following year a fellow returning from Gaultois reported seeing the clerk, cane in hand, completely blind!

The RCMP, on their first visit to Conne River by boat called at the home of Aunt Mary Louis in search of home brew. They found two quarters of moose taken out of season. The constables insisted on confiscating the meat, ignoring Mary's protests that her family needed it. She cursed them, swearing they would never leave the bay in their launch. Later that day the vessel developed engine trouble and was towed away.

A party of eight men rowed from Seal Cove to Bay de Nord to hunt caribou. They were met by an elderly Micmac woman whose husband they had employed as a guide on previous hunts. He was absent but was expected back shortly. Impatient, they set out on their own, confident they could manage. The woman became angry and warned that if they did not await her husband's return she would see to it they would not get any caribou. They left only to return several days later empty handed. They saw caribou but could not approach them. The following day, in the company of the guide who had since returned, they found that those same caribou were now approachable. They were convinced that the woman had "put a curse on them," asserting power over the caribou.

The shaman cured sickness. The Micmac perceived and treated disease as both physical and supernatural. The shaman administered medicines and invoked spirit forces in an elaborate curing rite. The shaman understood the medicinal properties of plants and herbs.[3] Among their preparations was one called "seven sorts":

> Perhaps the most interesting part of Micmac magic is connected with the mystic and medicinal herbs. Seven of these are boiled together in water [to] constitute a magical healing potion of great potency. The ingredients of this are: Alum bark (*vikpe*), hornbeam (*owelikch*), beeches (*soomooseeel*), wild willow (*elemojeechmokse*), wild blackberry (*waqwonuminokse*), ground hemlock (*kastuk*), red spruce (*kowotmonokse*). . . . All these ingredients must be gathered in autumn, otherwise the mixture will be worthless. Moreover, they must be gathered in the order given. The bark of the first five is used, and the roots of the last two. The trunk of every tree is divided into four sections sup-

> posed to face the sun between sunrise, at dawn, noon, sunset and midnight. In the forenoon one should cut the bark from the direction of sunrise as far as the direction of the sun at noon, but no further. This is the most propitious quarter, hence medicine gathered from it will yield the best results. In the afternoon cut from the noon point to the sunset point. This quarter is propitious, though less so. Bark gathered from the other two quarters from the right quarter at the wrong time is at least useless, often poisonous. For the sunlight purifies the side it touches, but the shadow is hostile to life. The roots should extend from the trunk towards the propitious side. This medicine is used both externally and internally.[4]

A student of Micmac folk medicine was told by Conne River informants:

> To make the medicine you must take equal amounts of the bark of the seven trees. It must be the inside bark of the cherry tree. The bark must be steeped in water for internal use. For external purposes, the mixture should be boiled until a black, molasses-like substance appears. This substance can be smeared on brown paper and applied in plaster form to the body. It is effective for healing or curing broken bones, bruises, or any kind of ailment.[5]

People testify that the "plaster moves over the body of its own accord, in the direction the pain or ailment takes, as it leaves the body."[6]

Shamans were those who demonstrated an ability to manipulate the supernatural, but everyone had access to the knowledge and power of the spirit world. Individuals acquired their *puoin* through "power quest":

> . . . generally, when a Micmac wishes to gain his power, he must, while keeping his object a secret, go into the woods alone and dwell there. His camp must be constructed to shelter two, and in all his equipments he must likewise provide for two. Even at his meals he must set apart an equal share for an unexpected visitor. At length he will find his food already cooked, upon his return to camp, and soon after he will begin to observe a faint and shadowy being flitting in and out of the wigwam. Gradually he will see this being more and more . . . clearly, until it grows as plainly visible as any man. Then the two will become friends and companions, and the Micmac will receive the gift of magic power.[7]

They then adopted *ntiomel* to embody the acquired power.

Dreams, avenues to the spirit world, were carefully examined for content. Elders recall the importance "old people" attached to dreams and how they interpreted them to divine the future. Another means of divination involved burning caribou bones: the resulting cracks were interpreted as the topographical features where game could be found.

The hunter was bound by rules and rituals governing his relationship with prey. Hesketh Prichard learned that

> . . . no Micmac hunter will ever kill a caribou stag without first whispering a short speech or prayer addressed to it in which he regrets the hard necessity that compels him to fire the death shot. [He will also add] his good wishes for the caribou in that land.[8]

The prayer reflected the hunter's dependence on the goodwill of fellow creatures, an admission that hunting success was as dependent on the benevolence of the animal's spirit as on the hunter's skill. Animals were addressed with reverence. As Speck once reflected, to the Micmac hunting was a "holy occupation."

Respect was demonstrated following the death shot. Bear was believed to possess a particularly powerful spirit. Food prohibitions resulted from the spiritual relationship with game. Elders remember a ban on eating bear brain, a portion of the beaver's hind foot, and a gland called the "whistler" from a caribou's stomach. "Poor Uncle Steve Joe ate it once, nearly starved to death on the country. He couldn't see the deer but he could sure hear them. They just kept whistling at him." The *bidirontech*, a lumpy growth which occasionally appears in the neck of large stags had special significance as a good-luck charm.[9]

One of the most widely reported elements of Micmac spirituality is their veneration of the "Bay de Nord Holy Cross" as a religious shrine. Despite its Christian character, elements of faith associated with the cross suggest aboriginal spiritualism.

Southwest of Conne River at the mouth of Bay d'Espoir is a fiord the French named Bay de Nord (shown on current maps as North Bay). Along its indraft land rises abruptly in sheer cliffs. There is one place to land—a small beach near the head of the bay. The Benoit and Pullet families lived here before moving to Conne River.

Archbishop Howley visited the site:

> On reaching the top of this ravine, some four or five hundred feet above sea level, the mountain spreads out flat as a table land for miles in every direction. Generally the rock is covered with a thin layer of turf and sod, with some young starved rank grass growing here and there among the moss. In places, however, there are large patches of the rock exposed, and quite nude of any vegetation. They are worn quite smooth from the action of the weather. On one of those bare stretches about twenty feet square there is a rude cross of large sized stones, weighing perhaps from ten to twenty pounds each laid out on the surface of the rock as if it were fashioned from a gigantic rosary or prayer-beads. The cross is only crudely outlined yet quite obviously visible. No one alive can tell anything about the origin of this cross; it was there long before the time of the oldest inhabitants, and their fathers and grandfathers have the same to say. No one can tell when it was made or how, for there are no stones anywhere within miles of a similar kind from which it could have been made, and no means by which they could have been brought to this site. The cross is held in great veneration by the Micmac Indians.[10]

A contemporary of Howley, Rev. M. F. Power of Harbour Breton, was told that the cross was discovered 80 years earlier, around 1830, by a hunter:

> Nearby he saw a large cross ingeniously and superbly traced, with miniature pebbles, on the solid whinstone ledge. The old woodman hastened to report his find to his Chief, describing the cruciform as ancient and well past its century.
>
> The Indians of to-day, viewing the cross as a hallowed shrine, visit it with great respect and regard it with every reverence. The Indian guide will tell the curious pilgrim that the Almighty placed the sign of His Holy Rood to bless poor ''Injun mans'' and his avocations. May be so! Who can say?[11]

Fr. Chrestien Le Clercq, a Recollet priest who lived among the Gaspé Micmac in the 1660s and 1670s, discovered that they used a cross as an object of worship, a protector or emblem:

> They drew it, and wore it, religiously upon their bodies and their clothes: it presided over their council, their voyages, and the most important affairs of their nation.[12]

In 1685 Fr. Emmanuel Jumeau described Micmac tribal territory on a map of the Maritimes. At the Miramichi River, the major hunting ground of the Gaspésian Micmac, he marked sites where the tribe had raised a cross. The Recollet called the Miramichi Rivière de Ste Croix; the Gaspésian Micmac they referred to as Cross-Bearing Indians.

Le Clercq at the time of his arrival noted that the tribe's faith in the cross was waning:

> Since this Gaspésian nation of the Cross-bearer has been almost wholly destroyed, as much by the war which they have waged with the Iroquois, as by the maladies which have infected this land . . . these Indians have gradually relapsed from this first devotion of their ancestors.[13]

Are the crosses in Gaspé and the one Bay de Nord of common origin? Perhaps the *Sa'qewe'ji'jk*, included a number of Gaspésian Micmac who brought with them their ancestral faith in the cross. Melvin Jeddore of Conne River, a recent visitor to the Cross, tells:

> If you pick up one of those rocks lying there you will find a hollow or depression under it where it has been worn down—because of the wind I guess. Now it must have taken a long time to do that.

Micmac from all over the island travelled here. Those from Conne River usually journeyed by sea:

> Whole families come, from the hoary grandparents to the children in arms, or rather on backs, and they all scramble up the brook, sometimes at the risk of their lives. A kind of rough ladder of ropes and sticks is made with "cradles" or loops for the old people who are thus hauled up to the plateau. They then perform various religious devotions, going round the cross on their knees, reciting their rosaries. . . .[14]

The ritual is Christian. The Micmac believed it possessed strong protective and curative powers. Pilgrims made offerings of shells and coins in return for blessing. Some brought a stone to replace one of those making up the formation. The removed stone, "a charm," was placed in the home to guard against fire and misfortune. The lame, blind and sick who made the pilgrimage sought cures. The waters of a nearby brook (Cross Brook), said never to freeze or run dry, were believed to have a powerful healing effect. Other visitors* speak of the remains of crutches and canes

*See Gerald Penney, "The Micmac Cross of Bay de Nord," *Newfoundland Quarterly*, 1983, Summer, Vol. LXXIX, no. 1, pp. 35-36.

left by the cured. Mary Benoit of Conne River was cured of partial blindness as a child.

Le Clercq was told that Gaspésian Micmac adopted the cross as an object of worship "at a time when their country was afflicted with a very dangerous and deadly malady." Tribal elders were visited in a dream by "a man, beautiful as he could be . . . with a Cross in his hand." They were told:

> . . . to make Crosses like that which were shown them, and to present these to the heads of families with the assurance that if they would receive the Crosses with respect they would find these without question the remedy for all their ills.[15]

The elders followed his directions:

> And so it turned out in fact, for the sickness ended, and all the afflicted who used the Cross with respect were restored miraculously to health.[16]

The Micmac venerate St. Anne, mother of the Virgin Mary, as patron saint of their nation. For over three centuries they have celebrated her feast day, July 26th. The celebration of St. Anne's Day is not strictly Christian in origin. Aboriginal Micmac traditionally held a summer gathering at which the assembled chiefs would meet to make "treaties of friendship and treaties for the common good."[17] The association of this ceremony with the feast of St. Anne was unknowingly instigated when in 1628 French missionaries dedicated to St. Anne a chapel built at their Cape Breton mission.

Newfoundland Micmac, particularly those from the west coast, made annual pilgrimages to Chapel Island in Cape Breton to attend the festival. A Micmac from Pictou, interviewed in 1911, describes how they were received:

> When the canoes arrive at the shore of the visited settlement, all the people in the settlement go to the shore to welcome the visitors. The visiting men get into the water, to the depth of their chests. Before the party lands, the two chiefs greet each other. The visiting chief then sings the *neskawe't* song. When he begins to sing, the home chief lays an old flintlock (formerly a bow and arrow) on the shoulder of the visiting chief, and discharges it. The home people carry the canoes of the visitors and their crews onto the beach and far beyond. Two shots are fired for the chief, and one for each other man in charge of a canoe while they are

> each carried ashore. The people at the settlement erect wigwams to accommodate the visitors.[18]

Several days of feasting and ceremonial speeches followed. Dances and games were held, gifts were exchanged and marriages arranged. Christian elements were incorporated with the participation of a priest, the celebration of Mass, and a procession bearing a statue of St. Anne.

Late in the 19th century the Micmac of Conne River organized their own St. Anne's Day celebrations, the Harbour Breton priest presiding. A witness to the 1951 celebration describes the preparations:

> On the eve of the feast the faithful of St. Anne's settlement, Conne River, men, women and children vied with each other to decorate in gala attire the church itself, the beautiful statue in the Shrine of St. Anne and the smaller statue which is carried in procession. Garlands of wild flowers and shrubs were artistically arranged. The route of the procession along which St. Anne's statue would be carried in triumph was lined with trees and display of flags.[19]

At the entrance to the church an archway of boughs was constructed. On St. Anne's Day "the chapel bell rang out its vibrant call for the faithful to assemble." After Mass the congregation formed a procession outside:

> The statue of St. Anne, decorated for the occasion, was carried by four young ladies dressed in white, preceded by banner of the Holy Family and of the Blessed Virgin. The children formed a guard of honour along the route. Next came the celebrant, acolytes, choir and entire congregation. To the accompaniment of the "Ave Maria Stella" and other hymns this procession wended its way along the path specially prepared for it.[20]

Back in church, a series of prayers and hymns ended the ceremony. Then the community feasted and danced to fiddlers and accordion players.

St. Anne's Day was an important annual event, as eagerly awaited as Christmas. It was a time to wear your best clothes, a time for singles to court, for men and women to renew friendships. It gradually emerged as a celebration involving all residents of the bay.

Micmac celebration of Christmas was also explicitly Christian. A distinctive facet was the "burning of the junks." On Christmas

Eve families gathered in one family's house. Three junks of birch from the previous year were retrieved from storage by three men. One by one each junk was placed in the fire as the assembled recited prayers and hymns. When the last junk had burned to ash three new junks were put in the fire one by one. These were burned for a few minutes until they were thoroughly scorched. Each man prayed alone as his junk was burned. During the scorching one of the two standing by would shout a signal to a man outside the door who fired a gun. The ritual ended when the last junk was cooled, scraped of ash, and set aside for the next year.

* * * * *

> The Micmacs are remarkable for the fact they are the only Canadian tribe that ever used hieroglyphics or ideograms, as a means of acquiring religious and secular knowledge.[21]

One consequence of early Micmac association with French clergy was the adoption of a written language, an ideographic language invented by Le Clercq.[22] The aboriginal Micmac had no written language, but they kept records using conventionalized pictures or signs as an aid to memory. It was this use of mnemonics which inspired Le Clercq:

> . . . being much embarrassed as to the method by which I should teach the Indians to pray to God, I noticed some children were making marks with charcoal upon birch-bark, and were counting those with the finger very accurately at each word of prayers which they pronounced. This made me believe that by giving them some formulary, which would aid their memory by definite characters, I should advance more quickly. . . .[23]

His hieroglyphics or picture symbols, some Micmac, others his own, were used to transcribe the teachings of the church. The Micmac responded enthusiastically.

> They have so much readiness in understanding this kind of writing that they learn in a single day what they would never have been able to grasp in an entire week without the aid of these leaflets. . . . They preserve these instructive papers with so much care, and they have for them so particular an esteem, that they keep them very neatly in little cases of birchbark bedecked with wampum, with beadwork, and with porcupine quills.[24]

Le Clercq left for France in 1686 without a successor. The Micmac persisted, learning to read and write with the aid of leaflets left by the priest. Formal instruction was not resumed until the 1730s when Fr. l'Abbé Maillard developed an interest in Le Clercq's work and set about improving it. He expanded the symbols and transcribed new works. With his death in 1762 clerical interest again lapsed until 1866 when Fr. Christian Kauder published several religious books in hieroglyphic script. The Micmac fully adopted the system, preserving manuscripts for their self-education. The use of the hieroglyphics was abandoned in favour of Roman letters, a move started by another French expert on Micmac language, Fr. Pacifique of Restigouche. He produced and distributed Micmac translations of the Bible, catechisms, and published a monthly newspaper.

The Newfoundland Micmac maintained the self-education begun by Le Clercq. Manuscripts introduced by immigrant families, each a treasured possession, were commonly used for religious instruction. Prayers, hymns and Sunday services involved recitation of these materials. MacGregor found Conne River Micmac were fully literate in their language, in hieroglyphic or Roman script. Many families subscribed to Pacifique's newspaper. Children were taught to read and write. Boys were often instructed by their fathers on the country and in the skills of the hunter, trapper and woodsman.

NOTES

1. Howley, *The Beothucks*, p. 153.
2. Frederick Johnson, "Notes on Micmac Shamanism," *Man*, Vol. XVI, 1943, pp. 53-80.
3. The knowledge and practice of medicine was not confined to the shaman. There was also the "maker of medicine" who, while not a shaman, was a physician nonetheless. Laurie Lacey, *Micmac Indian Medicine* (Antigonish: Formac Limited, 1977), p. 11.
4. Stansbury Hagar, "Micmac Customs and Traditions," *American Anthropologist*, O.S. Vol. 8, 1895, p. 174.
5. Lacey, *Micmac Indian Medicine*, p. 60.
6. Ibid., p. 60.
7. Ibid., p. 12.
8. Prichard, *Hunting Camps*, p. 137.
9. Two sources refer to this *bidirontech*: Dahl, "Indian Scrape," p. 32; and Millais, *Untrodden Ways*, pp. 312-313.

10. Rev. M. F Howley, "The Micmacs," *Newfoundland Quarterly*, 1914, Volume XIII, no. 4, p. 29.
11. Rev. M.F. Power, "The Micmacs," *Newfoundland Quarterly*, Vol. IX, No. 4, 1910, p. 2-3.
12. Le Clercq, *Gaspésia.*
13. Ibid., pp. 151-152.
14. Howley, "Newfoundland Name-Lore," p. 29.
15. Le Clercq, *Gaspésia.*
16. Ibid.
17. Wallis and Wallis, *Micmac Indians*, p. 183.
18. Ibid., pp. 184-185.
19. Gordon Perry, "St. Anne's Feast," *Holy Cross Annual*, 2nd edition, 1951-52, pp. 15, 16.
20. Ibid., pp. 16, 17.
21. Rev. Stanley St. Croix, "The Micmacs of Newfoundland," in J. R. Smallwood, ed., *The Book of Newfoundland*, (St. John's: Newfoundland Book Publishers, 1937), Vol. 1, p. 285.
22. For a history of the hieroglyphics, see Rev. John Lenhart, *History of Micmac Ideographic Manual* (Sydney: Nova Scotia Communications Society, 1976).
23. Le Clercq, *Gaspésia*, p. 131.
24. Ibid., p. 126.

CHAPTER 11

Trade and traders — Threat to trapping areas and salmon rivers — Destructive role of religion and priests — Fr. Stanley St. Croix and the Chief — Logging and sawmilling — Bowater's — Confederation — Hydro development

Government, church, industry and society each played a role in the subjugation of Canadian Indians. Conne River was safe from serious intrusion throughout the 19th century; however, by the early decades of the 20th century, white society had to be reckoned with at ever closer quarters. Interactions between the two cultures were not all negative, but they nonetheless threatened the natives' cultural integrity.

Trading patterns altered in the 19th century, from historical connection with the French to English settlements along the south coast. By mid-century most furs went to Newman & Co. at Gaultois. Around 1900 Newman's established a subsidiary outlet at St. Alban's to service the bay's growing settler population. An alternative market was provided by trading schooners.

Many with whom the Micmac traded exploited them. Millais wrote that "very often the fur-traders encourage the Indians to drink as soon as they have concluded a deal, and cheat the unfortunate men if they once fall into their clutches."[1] Merchants controlled the fur trade as well as the fishery. They outfitted trappers on credit against the fur to settle the account. The merchant manipulated the value of pelts. John's curse on Newman's clerk was a response to this relationship.

Honest merchants existed, Millais wrote:

> Phillip Ryan is a somewhat remarkable character. For forty years he has been in the service of the Anglo-American Telegraph Company, and, as his work does not entail any arduous duties, he can spend his time in farming, sport, and in doing a little trade with the Indians. He is one of the only two men whom the Indians trust and have regular dealings with, and his fairness and kindness to those nomadic people have earned for him a reputation which is only shared by Mr. Leslie of Baie d'Espoir. It is no slur on his intelligence to say that he invariably gets the worst of a bargain, for he is of that rare kind which does not count success by the acquisition of money, but rather that he may do unto others as he would be done by. . . . To give an instance of Mr. Ryan's

> methods, it is enough to say that whenever he is absent from home, the key of his house is left under the door for any wandering Indian to find. The traveller may open and help himself to what he likes, taking flour, sugar, bacon, and tobacco. He lights a fire, stops in the house as long as he likes, and may not be there another year; and yet the owner never loses so much as a darning-needle, nor does the Indian fail to render to him an accurate account of the things he has taken, and to pay for them in the skins of foxes and otters.[2]

Ryan's station was a favourite haunt, particularly for those of the east country.

Another telegraph employee, Mr. Leslie, came to Bay d'Espoir in 1880 to operate the station. Like Ryan, he "isolated himself in this out-of-the-way corner of the earth quite voluntarily" at a time when there "were no inhabitants but the Micmac Indians, who dearly loved him for his honest dealings."[3]

Some traded further afield to obtain better prices. Matthew Jeddore, who trapped Little and Big Gull lakes, explains that he sometimes packed fur over Middle Ridge and down Terra Nova River. Andrew Joe and his neighbours in the west country sometimes continued to Bishop's Falls or Glenwood. If prices were poor they travelled by train to St. John's, returning by coastal boat.

For many years the Micmac made "the best kinda livin' " off the country. The fur market remained healthy. Trappers had little difficulty supporting families on their territory's yield. Even subjected to the merchant's devaluation fur fetched respectable prices.

Trade was not confined to fur. As woodsmen proficient with axe and crooked knife, the Micmac produced tubs, paddles, oars, axe handles, hammer handles and furniture from witch hazel and birch. Women traded woven baskets, hampers and boxes. Trade included food—hares, grouse, berries, trout, salmon, caribou, and later moose. Settler families would outfit a hunter for fresh meat.

Settler life blended primary agriculture, fishing, logging, hunting and trapping. Indian–white relations expanded beyond sporadic trade, the Micmac now competed for land and resources. Settlers generally respected Micmac rights, but a sawmill, which MacGregor mentioned, was built without tribal permission. A dispute arose over Conne Brook salmon. In the late 19th century a settler family on the opposite shore began fishing commercially under licence from Newman & Co. The Micmac could do little but watch the salmon supply dwindle.

An incipient threat to their interests on the country came from beyond Bay d'Espoir. An example was Jeddore's outburst when his territory was trapped by settlers ascending Gander River. Trappers working Terra Nova River encroached on the eastern territories. The country of the Johns and Bernards was frequented by settlers from Fortune Bay hunting caribou in winter. They were not clearly regarded as trespassers, for the families exclusive right was to fur-bearing animals only. Encounters on the country were common.

> So I was curious, as no Indians were about in our country, and white men never come in so far, especially in the winter. We crossed the brook, and I see at once that the track was a white man's, as he wore boots, that he was running, and that he warn't carrying no load, cos his footin' was light on the snow. "That feller's lost sure," says I to Micky, "and we must find him before night or he'll be dead."
>
> I takes my tomahawk and some rum and meat and we flies along the track, for the man was scared and going fast. The footing goes in big circles, and now and again we see where the feller had fell down and bite at the snow, so he was about done and going mad.
>
> "Hurry up, Micky," said I, "or we'll be too late." It was cold enough for frost-bite even with two pairs of mits, and when night came on, if a man fall and couldn't get up, he'd very soon die. But Micky was kind o' scared and say to me, "What if he jump on us and try to kill us; when a man's mad with fear he do most anything." But I show him the handle of my tomahawk, and meant to stun the feller if he try any tricks.
>
> The strength of that white man was considerable, for Micky and I had to run like deer on our rackets to gain ground, but by-and-by we see he was slowin' and fallin' oftener. Presently I sees his head poking out from behind a bush, so I shouts to him, and he rushes up to me and grabs me round the legs. Micky wanted me to hit him, but I knew he was only mad with joy. His name was Michael Fannell, and he said he thought he was going home. So he was—nearly.
>
> He was so done, with his boots and clothing all tore to pieces, that Micky and I had to carry him on our backs five miles to the tilt, but once there we rubbed him with rum, dressed him in our spare clothes, and soon had him asleep and comfortable.

> Three days afterwards we came with our man to a place about twenty miles above the Bay de Nord Mill, and there we meets a great company of men comin' to look for Michael Fannell.[4]

When asked what they would have done had Fannell been dead, Bernard replied, "I'd a brought out a piece of him anyway—his head perhaps." Millais explains:

> An Indian is fond of saying something gruesome just to see what the effect will be. These Newfoundland Micmacs do not like to be thought the savages many of the fisher folk consider them to be.[5]

Thus the relationship was somewhat ambivalent, the settlers sometimes prejudiced, sometimes appreciative. Power remarked, perhaps referring to others like Fannell, "the Micmac is often the object of grateful anecdotes amongst the white settlers whom he has befriended."[6]

The more accessible territories around Long Pond and the lower Salmon River were taken over by settlers. There is no record of disputes. Several west country families retreated, concentrating their efforts in the heart of the interior. Some, bachelor Noel Louis in particular, took non-native partners.

The Micmac were caught in a squeeze, their traditional territory pressured from all directions. Rights they believed theirs were no longer evident as boundaries blurred. Settler intrusions, though not persistent, reminded them of their vulnerability. A formal challenge to their rights was imposed through legislation.

Wildlife regulations, long a contentious issue with natives, were imposed from without, and were tailored to white interests. Colonial wildlife regulations governing caribou and salmon were precipitated by the drastic depletion of these resources. Caribou were critical to the Micmac, but incidental to settlers, most of whom were engaged in fishing and wage employment. The Micmac had a vested interest in preserving the basis of their livelihood. To them caribou seemed invulnerable, their immense herds beyond threat, their numbers on the increase.

Salmon, a more vulnerable resource, showed no appreciable reduction until European settlement and a commercial fishery began. Regulations setting the season, bag limits and methods of harvest for salmon and caribou made no provision for Micmac interests.

Micmac caribou hunters were usually beyond the reach of wardens. Efforts of the Fish and Game Board to control the settler hunt were inadequate and could not deal with enforcement in the heart of the country. Local wardens seldom went far inland to apprehend Indian 'poachers.' Peter Oliver of Bay St. George recalls with a chuckle his annual hide-and-seek with the warden, while Conne River hunters took caribou in accordance with traditional harvests.

Conne Brook was patrolled each summer by a district warden. Wardens reported, referring to "Conne River (Indian Settlement)," that "the great trouble here is with the Indians, who fancy they have almost exclusive *rights* to the river and estuary."[7] Spears and weirs were banned, and they could no longer fish as they traditionally had, at least not "legally." In theory such regulations were intended to protect the 'legitimate' fishery pursued by the sportsman and the commercial fisherman. A patrol commander reported that Collier, a commercial fisherman, "complains of the Indians poaching, and the Indians complain of his doing the same; they probably both poach."[8] A warden complained that "to keep an Indian from spearing Salmon, Trout and Eels, I believe you must take his arms off."[9]

* * * * *

The Christian church suppressed traditional faith and language, fractured ethnic identity and accelerated cultural deterioration usually through church-sponsored education and suppression of native language. A school was established in Conne River by the Harbour Breton parish in 1908. Classes were held in a log cabin "12 feet by 15 feet, by no means new, with a small stove and two little windows,"[10] the unfinished home of Louis John. The school instructed students in English only.

The Micmac accepted the institution only in obedience to the church. It was extraneous if not contrary to their interests. Boys attended to the age of nine or ten when they joined their fathers on the country for quite different but essential education. Girls remained home to acquire essential skills.

MacGregor was encouraged by the initial results. Ann Mathias, the first teacher, spoke Micmac. After her replacement in 1911 the parish appointed a succession of non-native teachers. They substituted English in daily conversation and in time the Micmac language was almost lost.

* * * * *

St. Ignatius Catholic church in St. Alban's, built in 1902, was occupied by various priests from Harbour Breton parish. In 1916, Fr. Stanley St. Croix was assigned to it. The parish included four communities: St. Alban's, St. Veronica's, St. Joseph's and Conne River.

In St. Alban's Father St. Croix is fondly remembered as able and dedicated, serving the parish well from 1916 to 1946. He imported oxen as draft animals for the logging industry, an innovation which greatly improved range and output; purchased looms in an effort to develop an indigenous handicraft industry; and under the auspices of the parish formed the St. Alban's Co-operative Society, which ran a sawmill and dry goods store.

The Micmac welcomed St. Croix, for his arrival ended a long isolation from their church. The new priest was known from previous visits, the first in 1911.

> We arrived in St. Alban's on February 1st. A few hours later there was a call to Conne River, three miles across the Bay.
>
> The young pastor was rather timid of the Micmacs, but I had to face the ordeal of going amongst them. Two tall Micmacs had come for me, so we left the house to make the journey. When we reached the Bay ice, there was a surprise for me. A sled was there with a little seat for me to sit on. The good Micmacs were pulling me over the ice at a great pace. A short distance ahead two other men were noticed on the ice. These men saluted the new priest, when he came up to them, and took hold of the hauling rope with the others. After a while it dawned on me that this had already been arranged. The Micmacs who came on the call had provided a long rope so that all the Micmacs of the settlement could join in hauling the new priest over the ice. On arrival at the settlement the Chief, Reuben Louis, came along with great dignity to salute me.[11]

The goodwill St. Croix initially cultivated with Micmac eroded in the face of his insensitivity. The events underlying the alienation and eventual confrontation between St. Croix and Chief Noel Jeddore are now difficult to determine. Given their staunch faith in the church and its priests, some elders refuse to discuss the affair, fearful they might say something that could be construed as critical of St. Croix.

St. Croix objected to a number of features of Micmac faith and ritual. Micmac Catholicism was a synthesis of aboriginal and French Catholic ideas. Faith in the Micmac Holy Cross, St. Croix judged "superstition," despite the fact that the church recognized similar shrines and their curative powers. The burning of the Christmas junks he condemned as pagan. Hymns and prayers in Micmac he felt were "going too far, [were] mocking God and the church," Joe Jeddore explained.

As parish priest he was responsible for school administration. He told teachers to strictly enforce the use of English in the classroom. Children were strapped if they reverted to Micmac, and he banned the use of Micmac in church.

He was offended by the community's social life, such as impromptu kitchen dances where teenagers flirted, and by acceptance of a "love child." He ordered young couples seeing each other for over three months to marry or terminate the relationship. (A middle-aged woman remarked, "I guess that's why so many of us married so young.") Anyone who offended his strict moral code was sternly lectured, barred from church, or threatened with damnation.

St. Croix did not visit regularly, preferring to have the Micmac attend church in St. Alban's. Whenever he did visit he held services in the home of a settler family rather than in their church. He resented emergency visits in winter because of the added effort of snowshoeing.

St. Croix' avoidance of their church was significant. It was maintained and administered by the Chief, his assistant and elders. Chief Jeddore, his brothers Steve and Joe, and other elders took pride in their church and community. Through service and example they provided leadership on matters of faith, ritual and tradition. Such leadership, even to assuming priestly responsibilities, was based on necessity for the Newfoundland Micmac.

This leadership threatened St. Croix. He could not hope to eliminate respect for the Chief and elders. The elders maintained tradition. St. Croix employed the unquestioned acknowledgement of his spiritual authority, and there was a minority, those who married in, who supported his efforts.

Confrontation between Chief and priest, according to Noel Jeddore's son Victor, was precipitated by an elder's plan to rebuild the church. They had arranged with a mill owner in Morrisville to exchange lumber for Micmac labour at a construction site. ''This made St. Croix very angry and he threatened to tear down any church built at Conne. He wanted St. Alban's to be the church centre.''[12] Chief Jeddore called a community meeting at the church to present his case. He stated that it would be a terrible sin to abandon their church, faith and language, saying ''There is murder in our hearts if we do this.'' Father St. Croix mistook this talk of murder as a threat to his life, as he wrote in 1937:

> In 1924 the pastor [St. Croix] abolished the office of chief. Since then the Micmacs have got along without a Chief. Poor Noel left the settlement in disgrace for his insubordination, for Cape Breton, where he still lives.[13]

The Chief's ''insubordination'' and ''disgrace'' are not explained, nor are the reasons for his decision to abolish the chieftainship. St. Croix took possession of the Chief's medal and hung it about the neck of the statue of St. Anne.

There was resistance. Andrew Joe was encouraged to assume the chief's office but he refused, fearing further conflict. In letters to the exiled family, others asked Noel or Victor Jeddore to return. Victor explained that he was afraid ''the Conne people would lose proof of their Indian status.''[14]

The community drew into itself. Amelia Joe, Andrew's widow, recalls how the affair ''broke the faith of the people, [how] the old people seemed to die off right quick after that.'' Several families left to settle in Cape Breton or elsewhere in Newfoundland. Responsibility for community affairs was delegated to an appointed ''church committee,'' and Conne River became a dependency of St. Ignatius. St. Croix pressed the Micmac to attend church in St. Alban's, offering a boat service across the bay. Sylvester Jeddore operated the boat for a time, but found that during Mass St. Croix ''abused us,'' ridiculing Indian culture and ways.

St. Croix' attitude toward natives was characteristic of that era. He was bound by ideals and convictions, subscribing to the assumption that Indian people would have to become fully assimilated. This was inevitable and desirable; he merely sought to accelerate that process in the belief that it was in their best interests.

St. Croix left an indelible mark on the community, a sense of inferiority. At his hand the Micmac were estranged from their culture.

But economic factors also undermined the practical value of Micmac culture. The fur trade depended on the demand for fur, not on skill as a trapper or the productivity of the territory. As long as there was demand for the "trappings" of affluence, prices remained high. Fur markets steadily declined from the 1920s through the 1940s, so trapping declined. The only alternative was logging.

Five mills, four powered by steam, operated in Bay d'Espoir in 1912. One in Conne River the Micmac resented but evidently could not remove.[15]

Mill operators outfitted loggers for two seasons of activity, fall-winter and spring-summer. Big timber was harvested during the winter, hauled by hand or by draft animal over the snow.

While fur prices remained high, Micmac involvement in logging was minimal, confined to a few weeks in the spring. A decline in fur markets forced greater commitment to logging, which replaced trapping as the main means of support. It was a poor substitute.

> I rowed over a raft of logs to Morrisville late one summer, logs we cut up Southeast that winter. My father was going in trapping so he told me to take them over. They were good sized logs so he said I should get 90¢ each, but John K. only offered 25¢. We argued a bit till he upped it to 50¢ but that was it; no more. I had to take it. If I'd rowed them somewhere else perhaps they'd be full up and I'd have to bring them back.

A backlog of winter logs limited demand for the smaller logs. " 'Boughs, just a bunch of boughs,' he'd say when I rafted some logs over. They weren't but what could I do but take his price?" With increased demand by late August, logs appreciated, but few Micmac could wait. They subsisted weekly, logging through Thursday, rafting on Friday, "settling up" on Saturday. "Sometimes you'd come away with no more than a pound of tea and a gallon of molasses."

It was hard labour, hauling logs by hand. Once the larger trees on the reserve were cut the men moved up Conne and Southeast brooks where they competed with mill crews. Nicholas Jeddore built a sawmill at the mouth of Southwest Brook. It was water-powered, built on the profits of trapping and supplied by community loggers. Later the mill was moved upstream, but the dam broke one spring, destroying the business.

Shortly after this, in 1922, St. Croix established the St. Alban's Co-operative Society. This mill issued booklets of 5¢ and 10¢ coupons rather than giving credit. These were exchangeable for goods at the co-operative's store. Church dues and donations were payable in coupons, and the church committee was instructed to charge coupons at socials, including St. Anne's Day. "I guess everyone worked for Fr. St. Croix at one time or another," recalls one elder.

Loggers migrated overland for the spring drives and summer cutting at Badger, Bishop's Falls, Gambo and Grand Falls camps. Some never returned, including some of the Joes and the descendants of Joe Bernard. No family could be supported by trapping, and logging was limited and unreliable through the mid-1930s as sawmills closed due to the depression. More and more turned to "the dole" for relief. Conne River was reduced to abject poverty and dependence.

The 1940s was a decade of change because of the second world war, the development of a pulpwood industry in the bay, and confederation. Twelve Conne River men joined the Newfoundland Overseas Forestry Unit, an army of lumberjacks in the forests of Scotland. In their late teens and early twenties, they were all in search of adventure and a decent dollar. Nick Jeddore returned from trapping one day, saw a recruitment notice in the store and decided to join up. The pay, $2 a day, was more than one could expect from logging or trapping. On their return most gave up trapping. Fur prices had hit rock bottom, and caribou were scarce. Muskrat was the only remaining pelt with any value.

In 1943 Bowater's built ten camps up Conne and Twillick brooks, each manned by 30 loggers. The season was brief, from June through August, as the cut was proportional to the carrying capacity of the brooks on the spring run. Pulpwood stockpiled along the river was dumped and run downstream to a massive boom built across the upper end of Conne Arm. From there it was rafted, towed through the gut, to Burnt Woods and loaded aboard freighters for Corner Brook. The operation lasted 15 years.

It was a sizable concern and provided partial relief from poverty and idleness, but work was seasonal. Better-paying jobs, timekeepers, cooks, scalers, and wage-employed loggers, were held by settlers; the Micmac were confined to short-term logging contracts, the spring drive and building the boom. With unemployment so widespread it was an employer's market. When ships arrived and the unemployed gathered to load pulpwood, the Micmac were chosen last.

The country life was essential during the 1950s and 1960s against this backdrop of poverty and unemployment. Each family needed food. While a few trapped, all picked berries, snared rabbits, fished and hunted as needed. Moose were introduced twice in Newfoundland. In 1885 a bull and cow were landed in Gander Bay. Charles Francis was hired to tend the pair. Upon their release they were shot by local hunters. A 1904 attempt at Howley was more successful. Much of the island is ideally suited to moose, and pulpwood clear-cutting operations left large areas of young browse. They multiplied rapidly and dispersed widely and by the mid-1930s had spread to Bay d'Espoir. They replaced caribou as the main meat in the Micmac diet by the 1950s.

Hunters quickly became familiar with their whereabouts and habits, particularly their winter yards. Men hunted singly or in teams. Special hunts involving up to 12 men were organized in preparation for Christmas. On a collective hunt they had their "gut feed" on the spot, saving the nose, tongue, liver and kidney for elders.

The most popular hunting area was Little River, around River Pond, about a ten-mile hike. Here some built small tilts where for periods during summer and fall whole families retreated. Moose, rabbit, trout, birds and berries were plentiful. Trappers were displaced from their traditional hunting grounds in the west country and subsistence activities, including moose and caribou kills, were now confined to the east. Wildlife officials informally acknowledged a special interest on the part of the Micmac. Certainly the local warden was known to look the other way. An informant recalls at a meeting in St. John's the chief warden directed those patrolling the Conne River area not to bother with local hunters.

Subsistence hunting fed the family, but employment provided housing and clothes. Guiding was a ready means of work for a few weeks of the year. Visiting sportsmen were not prepared to rough it by canoe and tent in the manner of Millais and company, but now expected air transportation and modern lodging as was provided by several outfitters after the war. Micmac guides were hired, among them Matty Jeddore, who served as head guide for several outfitters.

Few were employed, and jobs were something you pursued elsewhere, in logging and construction camps and, increasingly, on the mainland. Conne River Micmac worked as woodsmen and labourers, possessing few skills beyond those of the country. Education as a gateway to success had failed them as it had their fathers. By 1958 only 30 per cent were functionally literate; standards would rise slowly. The population rose dramatically to the point where the school could not handle the burden. Higher grades were eliminated by parish order and students were required to board at St. Alban's.

The community's pathetically inferior standard of housing was depressing. In the early days of the sawmill industry when fur prices were still high, people built and maintained fairly substantial homes. More common now were small one- and two-bedroom houses, home to families of eight, ten or more; many lacked water, sewage or heating.

The 1960s offered hope with a flurry of construction activity in the bay. From 1962 through 1966 new roads were built linking all communities near Conne River with the Trans-Canada Highway at Bishop's Falls. Conne River men were employed on road crews.

The Bay d'Espoir hydro project harnessing the Salmon River was a mammoth project. It generated jobs on the main dam at Long Pond, on various diversions and on transmission lines. It produced no more than a brief burst of activity. Spin-off industries failed to materialize and, after completion in 1967, the local economy again lapsed into stagnation.

One lasting impact of these developments on the land was an invasion of the country adjacent to the Harbour Breton road. Weekend hunters from St. Alban's, Hermitage Bay and other places had access to some of the best hunting and fishing areas on the island. Amateur trappers, joy-riding snowmobilers, and fly-by-night hunters have quickly, in Ron John's words, "torn up the country." Each summer dozens of weekend fishermen line Conne Brook, attracted by its reputation. The Bay d'Espoir highway and the Harbour Breton road fragmented the caribou. The former, bisecting the southern interior, inhibits the movement of the herd between the east and west country. Caribou in the east have been pushed northeast onto Middle Ridge. "We used to have a day's hiking to hit the country; now it's two hours," explains Ralph John. The road destroyed one of his trapping cabins and some traplines.

The hydro project flooded much land, caribou feeding and calving grounds and hunters' campsites. The fear of its long-term consequences prompted objection, but it ended hunting activity on the west country: "It's one big ocean now," as Larry Paul remarks. Long Pond, nearly doubled in size, now poses an obstacle more hazardous than it was in Joe Jeddore's day. In winter it takes longer to freeze. Snow machines and power boats are now needed to travel the west country. The project has had an impact on the east country also, where transmission lines slice across the travel routes, traplines and hunting grounds between Conne River and Meddonagonix.

In 1949 Newfoundland joined Canada. For Newfoundlanders it was a momentous decision hotly debated. Like thousands of "baymen" the Micmac hoped that union would alleviate poverty, buoyed by the knowledge that Nova Scotia Micmac were Indians under the British North America Act. The federal government was obliged to extend to Indian people certain rights, privileges, and protections. This historic and legal responsibility had evolved through the early period of English colonization and was entrenched in the Royal Proclamation of 1763.

The matter was discussed in Ottawa in 1947 when members of the Newfoundland delegation met with federal officials to draft terms of union. The resulting report included a specific recommendation to the effect that the federal government would proceed with the registration of native people under the Indian Act. This section was later omitted.* When questioned about this omission, Joey Smallwood explained that under the Indian Act Indian people did not have the right to vote, their registration in Newfoundland would have automatically disenfranchised them. This was the rationalization, but, when the Indian Act was amended in 1960 to enfranchise all native people, neither the federal nor the provincial government reconsidered Indian rights in this province.

In the 1960s a series of events unfolded which, like confederation, ought to have brought major benefits. It began with an exchange of letters between the provincial and federal authorities concerning Newfoundland's request for financial assistance to provide medical services to isolated Inuit of northern Labrador.

---

*See Edward Tompkins, "Pencilled Out: Newfoundland and Labrador's Native People and Canadian Confederation, 1947-1954," (unpublished paper, 1988).

From this emerged the "Federal Provincial Agreement on Indian and Inuit People." The federal government agreed to reimburse the province for 90 per cent of all funds extended to the Labrador Indian and for housing, education, economic development and health care.

NOTES

1. Millais, *Untrodden Ways*, pp. 224-225.
2. Ibid., pp. 265-266.
3. Ibid., p. 196.
4. Ibid., p. 300.
5. Ibid., p. 300.
6. Power, "The Micmacs," p. 4.
7. Henry Camp, "Annual Report," *JLC*, 1873, p. 405.
8. Captain Miller, "Report of the Fisheries," *JLC*, 1874, p. 392.
9. Camp, "Annual Report," 1873, p. 405.
10. Governor MacGregor, *Report on a Visit*, p. 3.
11. St. Croix, "The Micmacs," pp. 284-285.
12. Laurie Lacey, private communication of an interview with Victor Jeddore, 1979.
13. St. Croix, "The Micmacs," p. 286.
14. Ibid., p. 286.
15. See Cokes, *Spatial Patterns*, for an account of the sawmill industry in Bay d'Espoir.

Epilogue

A Chief and five councillors were elected in 1972 to form the Conne River Indian Band Council. A provincial organization, the Federation of Newfoundland Indians, formed in 1973, sought recognition of and registration for Newfoundland natives. Community-generated political action led to Conne River's inclusion in 1973 as a native community under a cost-shared federal/provincial agreement. A 1984 federal Order in Council registered Conne River Micmac under The Indian Act. In 1987 the Samiajij Miawpukek Indian Reserve, an enlargement of a colonial reserve, was created.

In 1993 there were 650 members of Miawpukek Mi'kamawey Mawi'omi. A direct funding agreement for community and economic development, school and health facilities (the only one in Atlantic Canada) was signed in 1985. Under it, band administration is accountable to members rather than the Indian Affairs department. The Miawpukek Band, while not free of internal conflicts, has been recognised as one of Canada's most progressive, in the forefront of the native self-government movement.

Acknowledgements

The author and editor express heartfelt appreciation to the Micmac of Conne River and other locations. We recognise the vision, personality and friendship of the late Bill Joe, whose enthusiasm for the project was largely responsible for its completion. On behalf of the many people who helped, advised and collaborated, we hope it fulfils his expectations.

Bay St. George Micmac

M. Miot, 1859

Conne River

F. Johnson, 1931

Frank Joe family and Peter Stride

F. Speck, 1922

Joe Jeddore

F. Johnson, 1931

Joe Jeddore and Matty Burke

F. Johnson, 1931

Nick and Melvin Jeddore, A. Clarke and Steve John

E. John, 1963

Jim John

PANL, 1930s

Caribou skin canoe

D. Quinton, 1981

Michael Joe, Sr.

Conne Arm

G. Penney, 1992

St. Anne's Church

G. Penney, 1992

Bill Joe, Freeman MacDonald, A. Benoit and Matty Joe

J. Wetzel, 1980

Aloysius Benoit

J. Wetzel, 1980

Martin Jeddore, Sr.

D. Quinton, 1981

Larry Jeddore and Martin Jeddore, Jr.

G. Penney, 1984

Molly McDonald and Matty Joe

G. Penney, 1992

Wilfred and Barbara Drew family

G. Penney, 1989

Amelia Joe

G. Penney, 1983

Bay de Nord Cross

G. Penney, 1982

St. Anne's Day procession

G. Penney, 1980

Mary Lewis

F. Johnson, 1931